A TEACHER'S GUIDE TO
Using the **Common Core
State Standards** With
Gifted and Advanced
Learners in the
English
Language Arts

A TEACHER'S GUIDE TO Using the **Common Core State Standards** With Gifted and Advanced Learners in the **English Language Arts**

Claire E. Hughes, Ph.D., Todd Kettler, Ph.D,
Elizabeth Shaunessy-Dedrick, Ph.D, and
Joyce VanTassel-Baska, Ed.D

A Service Publication of the

NATIONAL ASSOCIATION FOR
Gifted Children

PRUFROCK PRESS INC.
WACO, TEXAS

Library of Congress Cataloging-in-Publication Data

Hughes, Claire E., 1967-
 A teacher's guide to using the common core state standards with gifted and advanced
learners in the English/language arts / by Claire E. Hughes, Ph.D., Todd Kettler, Ph.D,
Elizabeth Shaunessy-Dedrick, Ph.D, and Joyce VanTassel-Baska, Ed.D.
    pages cm
 Includes bibliographical references.
 ISBN 978-1-61821-104-0 (pbk.)
 1. Language arts--Standards--United States--States. 2. Gifted children--Educa-
tion--United States. I. Title.
 LB1576.H76 2013
 808'.042071--dc23
                              2013023454

Edited by Rachel Taliaferro

Production design by Raquel Trevino

ISBN-13: 978-1-61821-104-0

Prufrock Press Inc.
P.O. Box 8813
Waco, TX 76714-8813
Phone: (800) 998-2208
Fax: (800) 240-0333
http://www.prufrock.com

Table of Contents

Acknowledgements

Many people have assisted with the efforts in developing this book. They include the leadership of NAGC, the NAGC Professional Standards Committee, reviewers, NAGC staff, and experts who were a part of the development of the other books in this series on using the Common Core State Standards with gifted and advanced learners.

We would like to thank Paula Olszewski-Kubilius, NAGC president, and the NAGC Board, who have understood the urgency for responding to the Common Core State Standards and the gifted education community's need to have a voice in their implementation. From the beginning, the NAGC Professional Standards Committee also has been actively involved in providing the framework, expertise, and support for this book. Moreover, the NAGC leadership group also includes Nancy Green, executive director of the NAGC, and NAGC Association Editor Carolyn Callahan, who have supported the development process and the need for this book.

This book has also been strengthened through a rigorous review process. We want to thank these reviewers from the NAGC Publications Committee who took time to provide valuable advice and feedback and Felicia Dixon, Elizabeth Fogarty, William D. Keilty, Penny Kolloff, and Vicki Vaughn for their input on the manuscript. We also want to thank again the authors and contributors from the first book: Susan K. Johnsen, Jennifer L. Jolly, and Debra A. Troxclair.

Finally, the authors want to express a special thank you to Jane Clarenbach, Director of Public Education at the NAGC office, who has provided the needed energy in supporting the authors through the process and a critical eye in editing the many drafts of this book. She has shepherded this writing project with great diplomacy, tact, and endless amounts of patience.

Claire Hughes
Todd Kettler
Elizabeth Shaunessy-Dedrick
Joyce VanTassel-Baska

Foreword

Only a year has passed since the National Association for Gifted Children's (NAGC) first two books about using the Common Core State Standards and gifted and advanced students were published. Urgently requested from all corners of the NAGC membership, the two books, one focused on mathematics and the second on English language arts, have been well received by the NAGC membership and beyond. Although the 46 states that have adopted the CCSS seem to face a wide range of implementation phases and challenges—some advancing rapidly, others mired in state politics—the demand for guidance about the relationship between the CCSS and gifted programming remains strong.

That is why it made so much sense for NAGC leaders and subject matter experts to convene once again in Washington, DC, to consider additional materials to respond to feedback from convention attendees, state directors of programs for the gifted, and educators in the trenches. It was clear that something more was needed.

Although the first books help educators understand how to approach differentiation of student assignments under CCSS for learners who meet the standards earlier and faster, the two new teachers' guides to using the Common Core State Standards with gifted and advanced learners provide an even more practical orientation. The new books include additional examples of differentiated learning experiences at key grade levels within specific strands of the CCSS. They also include examples of assessments that will be helpful in evaluating more complex and creative performance. Beyond providing additional resources, the books also feature a discussion of scope and sequence and how instructional practices for high-ability learners can be integrated in the classroom.

Clearly, the CCSS hold great promise for better teaching and learning, and they have stimulated a national conversation about what shape these improvements can and should take. With these high-quality, carefully crafted publications on how the CCSS should be implemented for gifted and advanced learners, NAGC has contributed significantly to this national conversation. These books not only serve as useful resources for teachers in the classroom, they also clearly demonstrate why grade-level curriculum and instruction are simply not enough to challenge our nation's gifted and advanced learners.

Testing, accountability, and teacher training seem to be the next frontier now that nearly all of the states have adopted the CCSS. On that front, NAGC has a head start, thanks to these books. Professional development based on the chapters and examples outlined in these pages will equip teachers with the knowledge and skills to meet the challenges of the CCSS. As a result, the gifted community is well positioned to successfully take the next steps with implementation.

We can't say enough about how remarkable it is that a key group of leaders and experts came together not once, but twice in service to gifted learners and the teachers who support them. The CCSS workgroup and others who provided input on the two books once again deserve recognition and appreciation, particularly NAGC Professional Standards Committee cochairs Susan Johnsen and Joyce VanTassel-Baska and their coauthors

Susan Assouline, Elizabeth Shaunessy-Dedrick, Claire Hughes, Todd Kettler, and Gail Ryser.

The impact of this work on gifted education, classroom practice, and on the knowledge and skills of gifted teachers, as well as those who work in heterogeneous classrooms, will be felt greatly in the years to come. For the National Association of Gifted Children, there is no greater mission.

Paula Olszewski-Kubilius
NAGC President, 2011–2013

Nancy Green
NAGC Executive Director

Introduction

The purpose of this second book on using the Common Core State Standards for English Language Arts (CCSS-ELA) with advanced and gifted learners is to provide classroom teachers and administrators examples and strategies to implement the new standards for advanced learners at all stages of development across the years in K–12 schools. One aspect of fulfilling that purpose is to clarify what advanced opportunities look like for such learners from primary through secondary grade levels. How can schools provide the level of rigor and relevance within the new standards as they translate them into experiences for gifted learners? How can they provide creative and innovative opportunities to learn what will nurture the thinking and problem solving of our best students in the subject area?

This second book also serves as a primer for basic policies and practices related to advanced learners in school. At all levels, schools must be flexible in the implementation of policies related to acceleration, waivers, and course credit, all of which may impact gifted learners. The developers of the CCSS-ELA acknowledge that advanced learners may move through the standards more readily than other learners (National Governor's

Association Center for Best Practices & Council of Chief State School Officers [NGA & CCSSO], 2010), attesting to the importance of using differentiated approaches for these learners to attain mastery and/or progress in academic achievement at their level. It is critical that schools allow for flexibility in these areas and others in order to accommodate our advanced learners.

In this book, we also want to demonstrate vertical planning in the language arts that lends vision to the work of teachers as they deliver classroom instruction at one level but prepare students for the succeeding levels in the journey toward the real world of language-based careers. What is the progressive development of skills, habits of mind, and attitudes toward learning needed to reach high levels of competency and creative production in language-related fields? We have included a model scope and sequence of these talent activities in the language arts that school districts may use to plan appropriate differentiated experiences for advanced learners at all stages of development.

This book, like the first one (VanTassel-Baska, 2013), is based on a set of underlying assumptions about the constructs of giftedness and talent development that underpin the thinking that spawned the CCSS-ELA work. These assumptions are:

- Giftedness is developed over time through the interaction of innate abilities with nurturing environmental conditions. Thus, the process is developmental, dynamic, and malleable.
- Many learners show preferences for particular subject matter early and continue to select learning opportunities that match their predispositions if they are provided with opportunities to do so. For many children, especially those in poverty, schools are the primary source for relevant opportunities to develop domain-specific potential, although markers of talent development also emerge from work done outside of school in cocurricular or extracurricular contexts.
- Aptitudes may emerge as a result of exposure to high-level, challenging activities in an area of interest. Thus,

teachers should consider using advanced learning activities and techniques as a stimulus for all learners.

- In the talent development process, there is an interaction effect between affect and cognition, leading to heightened intrinsic motivation of the individual and focus on the enjoyable tasks associated with the talent area. This dynamic tension catalyzes movement to the next level of advanced work in the area.

- Intellectual, cultural, and learning diversity among learners may account for different rates of learning, different areas of aptitude, different cognitive styles, and different experiential backgrounds. Working with such diversity in the classroom requires teachers to differentiate and customize curriculum and instruction, always working to provide an optimal match between the learner and her readiness to encounter the next level of challenge.

Thus, users of this book need to be sensitive to the ideas contained herein as not being intended to apply exclusively to identified gifted students but also to those students who show an interest and readiness to learn within the domain of English language arts. Therefore, students with high potential and advanced readers would be candidates for a differentiated ELA curriculum, as would students from poverty and twice-exceptional learners.

The decision to provide examples for advanced learners and to employ that terminology was made with an eye to the mixed group of students who may benefit from advanced instruction in language arts. This group would include high-level readers, high achievers in the language arts area, as well as identified gifted learners. We have not made distinctions about curriculum options within those groups and as a result, the examples may not be sufficiently differentiated for some gifted learners, while they may be too demanding for some high achievers within a given period of time.

Finally, it is our hope that the book provides a roadmap for meaningful state and local educational reform that elevates learning in English language arts to higher levels of rigor for gifted and, indeed, all learners who can benefit from the elevation of learning experiences suggested.

As in the first book, the authors believe there are certain foundational understandings that readers need to have in order to understand the adaptations suggested in this book. These common understandings relate to what the Common Core State Standards are, the rationale for differentiating them for gifted learners, how they relate to 21st century skills, how they align with gifted education standards, and the key strategies we may use to differentiate these standards effectively for our target population. Thus, these sections have been reproduced here from the first NAGC CCSS-ELA book (VanTassel-Baska, 2013) to aid new readers in this understanding.

The Common Core State Standards for English Language Arts: What Are They?

The Common Core State Standards for English language arts (CCSS-ELA) are K–12 content standards that illustrate the curriculum emphases needed for students to develop the skills and concepts required for the 21st century. Adopted by 46 states to date, the CCSS are organized into key content strands and articulated across all years of schooling and, in most cases, replace the existing state content standards. The initiative has been state-based and coordinated by the National Governors Association (NGA) and the Council of Chief State School Officers (CCSSO). Designed by teachers, administrators, and content experts, the CCSS are intended to prepare K–12 students for college and the workplace.

The new CCSS are evidence-based, aligned with expectations for success in college and the workplace, and informed by the successes and failures of the current standards and international competition demands. The new standards stress rigor, depth, clarity, and coherence, drawing from the National Assessment of Educational Progress (NAEP) Frameworks in Reading and Writing (National Assessment Governing Board [NAGB], 2008, 2010). They provide a framework for curriculum development work, which remains to be done although many states are already engaged in the process. States such as Indiana, Minnesota, Illinois, Georgia, and Maine are working within and across local districts to design relevant curriculum and to align current practice to the new standards.

Rationale for the Work

The adoption of the Common Core State Standards (CCSS) in almost every state is cause for gifted education as a field to reflect on its role in supporting gifted and high-potential learners appropriately in the content areas. As a field, we have not always differentiated systematically in the core domains of learning, but rather focused on interdisciplinary concepts, higher level skills, and problem solving, typically across domains. With the new CCSS, it becomes critical for us to show how we are differentiating for gifted learners within a set of standards that are reasonably rigorous in each subject area.

It has been stated by some that the CCSS-ELA core does not require any special differentiation for the gifted, and may obviate the need for gifted education services because the standards are already high level. Unfortunately, although the standards are strong, they are not sufficiently advanced to accommodate the needs of most gifted learners. As the CCSS developers have noted, some students will traverse the standards before the end of high school (NGA & CCSSO, 2010, p. 6), which will require educators to provide advanced content for them. Beyond accelerative methods, however, there is also a need to enrich the standards by ensuring that there are open-ended opportunities to meet the standards through multiple pathways, more complex thinking applications, and real-world, problem-solving contexts. This requires a deliberate strategy among gifted educators to ensure that the CCSS-ELA are translated in a way that allows for differentiated practices to be employed with gifted and high-potential students.

As with all standards, new assessments likely will drive the instructional process. Educators of the gifted must be aware of the need to differentiate new assessments that align with the CCSS-ELA as well. Gifted learners will need to be assessed through performance-based and portfolio techniques that are based on higher level learning outcomes than the new CCSS-ELA may employ.

Although the new CCSS-ELA are a positive movement for all of education, it is important to be mindful of the ongoing need to differentiate appropriately for our top learners within them. As a field, it is also critical that we agree on the need to align with this work so our voices are at the table as the CCSS-ELA become one important basis, along with the newly revised InTASC Model Teacher Standards (CCSSO, 2011) for elevating teacher quality and student learning nationwide.

Alignment to 21st Century Skills

This book includes a major emphasis on key 21st century skills (Partnership for 21st Century Skills, n.d.) in key activities and assessments employed in the examples. Several of these skill sets overlap with the differentiation emphases discussed below in relation to the gifted standards.

The skills receiving major emphases in the book examples include:

- *Collaboration:* Students are encouraged to work in dyads and small groups of four to carry out project activities, to discuss readings, and to plan presentations.
- *Communication:* Students are encouraged to develop communication skills in written, oral, visual, and technological modes.
- *Critical thinking:* Students are provided with models of critical thought that are incorporated into classroom activities, questions, and assignments.
- *Creative thinking:* Students are provided with models of creative thinking that develop skills that support innovative thinking and problem solving.

- *Problem solving:* Students are engaged in real-world problem solving and learn the processes involved in such work.
- *Technology literacy:* Students use technology in multiple forms and formats to create generative products.
- *Information media literacy:* Students use multimedia to express ideas and key learnings.
- *Cross-cultural skills:* Students read and discuss works and events representing the perspectives of different cultures and people.

Because these skills are relevant to all learners, the way they are addressed in the differentiation examples in this book (see page 35 and page 83) is important for educators to see the translation of the skills at higher levels and at earlier stages of development for gifted learners.

Alignment of the CCSS-ELA With the Gifted Education Programming Standards in Assessment, Curriculum Planning, and Instruction

This book, designed around the CCSS-ELA for use by teachers with advanced and gifted learners, was developed in alignment with not only 21st-century skills, but also with the *NAGC Pre-K–Grade 12 Gifted Programming Standards* (2010) in key areas and is connected and integrated in important ways to multiple professional communities, both within gifted education and across general education.

The NAGC Programming Standards (2010) represent the professional standards for programs in gifted education across Pre-K–12 levels. Within these standards, the curriculum and assessment standards were used to design the English language arts book in the following ways:

- *Development of scope and sequence:* The book has demonstrated a set of interrelated emphases/activities for use across K–12, with a common format and within key content strands.
- *Use of differentiation strategies:* The book developers used the central differentiation strategies emphasized in the standards including critical and creative thinking, problem-solving, inquiry, research, and concept development.

- *Use of acceleration/advancement techniques, including preassessment, formative assessment, and pacing:* The book developers used all of these strategies as well as advanced literature (advanced problem sets) to ensure the challenge level for the gifted.
- *Adaptation or replacement of the core curriculum:* The project extends the CCSS-ELA by ensuring that gifted learners master them and then go beyond them in key ways. Some standards are mastered earlier (e.g., reading and language skills), while others are practiced at higher levels of skill and concept.
- *Use of culturally sensitive curriculum approaches leading to cultural competency:* The book developers have employed world and multicultural literature to ensure that students have an appreciation for the contributions of different cultures to the literary canon.
- *Use of research-based materials:* Book developers have included models and techniques found to be highly effective with gifted learners in enhancing critical thinking, literary analysis, and persuasive writing. They have also used the questioning techniques found in Junior Great Books (Great Books Foundation, n.d.a) and the William & Mary language arts program (Center for Gifted Education, n.d.), both research-based language arts programs used nationally for the gifted learner.
- *Use of information technologies:* The examples provided suggest the use of visual media, computer technology and multimedia in executing the learning activities developed.
- *Use of metacognitive strategies:* The book developers included activities where students use reflection, planning, monitoring, and assessing skills.
- *Use of community resources:* The book includes opportunities for students to learn from a panel of experts or to interview a relevant person central to understanding some aspect of a given unit of study.

- *Development of career pathways:* Book examples include biography and autobiography as deliberate tools for students to model on an eminent person in the language arts such as a poet, novelist, or orator.
- *Talent development in areas of aptitude and interest in various domains (cognitive, affective, aesthetic):* The book presents examples that provide multiple opportunities for students to explore domain-specific interests such as writing, viewing, and oral expression; and exercising multiple levels of skills in cognitive, affective, and aesthetic areas.

Differentiating the CCSS-ELA for Advanced and Gifted Learners

Differentiation is based on an understanding of the characteristics of gifted and high–potential students *and* the content standards within a domain. The new Common Core State Standards provide an opportunity for the field of gifted education to examine its practices and align them more fully to the NAGC Programming Standards (2010) for curriculum, instruction, and assessment. Because the gifted programming standards in curriculum require us to engage in two major tasks in curriculum planning—alignment to standards in the content areas and the development of a scope and sequence—using the CCSS-ELA is a natural point of departure. The effort must occur in vertical planning teams within districts and states in order to ensure consistency and coherence in the process. There are four major strategies that may be employed to accomplish this task for gifted education.

Provide pathways to accelerate the CCSS-ELA for gifted learners. Some of the CCSS-ELA address higher level skills and concepts that should receive focus throughout the years of schooling, such as a major emphasis on the skills of argument. However, there are also more discrete skills that may be clustered across grade levels and compressed around higher level skills and concepts for more efficient mastery by gifted students.

Provide examples of differentiated task demands to address specific standards. Standards such as the research standard in English language arts lend themselves to differentiated interpretation by demonstrating what a typical learner on grade level might be able to do at a given stage of development versus what a gifted learner might be able to do. The differentiated examples should show greater complexity and creativity, using a more advanced curriculum base in English language arts. Although typical learners might learn the parts of speech and practice their application across grades K–8, gifted learners might instead explore the relationship of these parts of speech and their function in different sentence patterns at an earlier stage of development. Other degrees of differentiation may take place by adding complexity to the tasks and using enrichment techniques that address student needs and district demographics.

Create interdisciplinary product demands to elevate learning for gifted students and to efficiently address multiple standards at once. Because English language arts and mathematics standards can be grouped together in application, much of the project work that gifted educators might already use could be revised to connect to the new CCSS-ELA and show how multiple standards could be addressed across content areas. For example, research projects could be designed that address the research standard in English language arts and the data representation standard in mathematics by (a) delineating a product demand for research on an issue, (b) asking researchable questions that require quantitative approaches, (c) using multiple sources to answer them, (d) collecting data, (e) interpreting data, and then (f) representing findings in tables, graphs, and other visual displays that are explained in text and presented to an audience with implications for a plan of action. Such a project might also be possible for the gifted learner at an earlier grade than for a typical learner.

Create differentiated assessments to demonstrate gifted student authentic learning. The use of alternative assessments to calibrate the extent to which gifted students are performing at appropriately advanced levels in the areas of the language arts is also a critical consideration in differentiating the CCSS-ELA. The language arts curriculum should employ high-quality, performance-based pre- and postassessments to ensure that growth is being attained in higher-level skills and concepts. The use of product assessment for long-term work coupled with annual writing and literary analysis pre- and postassessments should be used to justify differentiated curriculum and instruction. Critical thinking and creative thinking growth should also be assessed.

In this second CCSS-ELA book, we focus primarily on the second strategy above, examples of differentiated task demands, in order to provide educators guidance in adapting the standards for advanced learners.

Creating Examples in English Language Arts for Advanced Learners

The examples that follow address important standards in reading that need to be differentiated for gifted and advanced learners at key stages of development. The processes to accomplish that task are noted, along with ideas for implementation and assessment.

In the first book on differentiating the standards (VanTassel-Baska, 2013), we focused on explicating standards by strand and across grade level clusters, providing exemplars for differentiating a reading standard for both literature and informational text, a writing standard for persuasive, narrative, and informational text, a speaking/listening standard, and a language standard for both grammar and usage. This text focuses on integrating writing and speaking/listening strands into the reading standards for literature and informational text through organizing multipart activities. The book also attends to four important strands within the reading standards.

Accelerated Reading and the Provision for Off-Level Materials

Another underlying differentiation feature of this guide is the judicious use of off-level reading material for the gifted at all stages of development. In general, all text selections have been considered for their Lexile level of 1–2 grade levels above the designated grade level band and/or their level of complexity of language and thought. Resources that have consistently been used in the gifted community to locate such texts are referenced in this document as well (e.g., *Books for the Gifted Child* and *Some of My Best Friends are Books*). Thus, by addressing the range, quality, and complexity of texts in the examples provided, this book addresses Standard 10, as gifted learner expectations are then raised correspondingly for Grades 3, 5, 8, and 10 by the 1–2 grade level consideration.

Furthermore, it is important to ensure that the use of primary source documents supersedes the use of secondary sources, particularly in the informational text standards. The use of original speeches, seminal documents, and artifacts such as diaries and letters is encouraged and reflected in the examples provided for advanced learners, further addressing issues surrounding text selection, range, quality, and complexity.

In the literature standards, the use of classical texts is favored over the use of children's and adolescent literature that may have little lasting value. The use of varied genres encourages the scope of reading so the employment of poetry, myth, fable, and short stories contributes to exposure and appreciation of multiple forms of literature. Moreover, the use of genres that are geared toward short selections favors the depth of reading required for sufficient analytical work by students, even those who are advanced readers.

Consideration for the interest of advanced readers for certain genres, authors, and specific works should also be considered in the selection of texts. Activity archetypes may be held constant while more individualized reading selections can be made.

Independent reading of advanced learners should focus on their interest levels but be balanced with challenging choices that provide a broad scope of reading materials.

Proficiency in reading for the gifted may best be judged through an assessment of reading comprehension and critical reading behaviors—and not through an assessment fluency, as many of these readers come to school already fluent beyond current age and grade placements. Consequently, the use of silent reading time, mandated in many school settings, may be targeted toward these skills through the use of center-based activities, book discussion groups, and reflective writing, all based on a recent reading.

The Examples in This Book

The learning experience examples that are provided in the next section of this book share some common features in respect to how the authors have chosen to represent them as well as how the task demands were conceptualized.

Off-level reading selections. The decisions to focus on the reading standards of both informational text and literature were derived from a consideration of what is essential to provide advanced readers in a reading program, namely appropriate off-level reading materials that are rich in language and thought. Once text selections are carefully made, task demands can be constructed around those texts that integrate the other CCSS-ELA standards of language, writing, and speaking and listening. In the informational text strand, choices of text were made in order to enhance interdisciplinary reading in the history and science content areas. In order to demonstrate this integration and interdisciplinarity appropriately, each set of task demands has three parts: Part I is typically a reading and discussion of the text selection; Part II is a writing assignment, linked to the selected reading in some way; and Part III constitutes a project assignment and/or an in-class presentation related to the example text. Thus, the reading standards are aligned to both writing and speaking standards within the CCSS-ELA framework. Text selection may be informed by the individual learner's needs and capacity and should be considered in collaboration with families and students. Teachers may wish to consult the references in the resource section of this guide for alternative reading selections.

Selection of targeted standards in reading literature and informational text. The selection of the standards within the CCSS-ELA that the authors emphasized was based on their criticality to being differentiated for the gifted learner. Because there is a parallelism between informational text and literature standards, the authors selected corresponding standards in each strand. Moreover, we selected standards not represented in the first language arts book. Thus, in this text, we focus on four strands in each standard that address the key components of

- citing the main idea and providing supporting evidence from text sources;
- describing the importance of time sequence in understanding text;
- establishing text meaning through the use of words and phrases; and
- engaging in the comparative analysis of texts in respect to key elements.

In addition, by addressing text complexity, range, and quality, which are specifically addressed in Standard 10, the total number of standards addressed in this book is five.

Attention to the scope and sequence of the CCSS-ELA. The literature and informational text standards were analyzed for how they became more complex as students matured from primary to intermediate to middle school and high school levels. Tables were constructed that annotate the important distinctions found in the standards as students move from K–12. In this way, teachers can easily see that the choice we made to focus on anchor grade levels was driven by the sameness of the standard across grade level bands and to emphasize the implications for allowing advanced readers to traverse the scope and sequence of the standards at a faster pace than other learners. We also have created a programmatic scope and sequence chart that coalesces all of the language arts learning components in order to view the talent development trajectory. It is essential that educators keep the scope and sequence progression in mind in planning for the advanced learner who will continue into college and beyond with a more advanced conceptual and skill-based toolkit for work in the professions.

Organization of the Examples

At the end of each learning experience example, provided by standard and strand, there is a brief description of how the standard-based activity set has been differentiated for advanced readers and learners beyond accelerating the reading level of text selections. In most instances, the approaches used included greater complexity, greater depth, and more creativity. There is also a section on implementation that provides the reader ideas for making the learning experiences work in the classroom. Finally, the examples provide assessment ideas for use in the classroom that relate to the example tasks.

The organization of task demands is presented in a comparative structure that allows the reader to examine a task demand that addresses the standard for typical learners at the grade level band designated. The typical learner examples were often found in online materials on the CCSS-ELA from states or the CCSS-ELA developers. Sometimes they were constructed from more advanced activities. The advanced learner examples were pulled or adapted from existing research-based materials that are differentiated for the gifted or created by the authors themselves.

The approach to differentiation. The differentiated learning experiences provided are intended to represent the use of key features of differentiation as described in each example. They are not meant to convey the greatest amount of differentiation that could be employed, to represent all of the forms of differentiation available for use by teachers, or to be sufficiently differentiated for all gifted learners. The main value in the learning task examples is to provide teachers a pathway to more advanced instructional approaches around a given standard. Not only are the examples not as differentiated as they might be in all respects, they are differentiated to align to a given common core standard. We have deliberately not gone beyond the standard to address the nature of the higher level tasks. If the standard calls for analysis, for example, we have used analysis as the higher level thinking skill focus, and have not necessarily added on additional higher level thinking skills. We also have not differentiated for differentiation's sake if we judged the typical learner example to be reasonably appropriate for advanced learners as well.

The differentiation of the curriculum in these examples probably will require more work for advanced students, given the multilayered approach of infusing writing, speaking, and listening into each learning experience provided. Employing greater depth, complexity, and creativity in a curriculum in language arts does require more work in thinking and in production. Such work will enhance students' habits of mind in engaging critically and creatively with what they read, and producing ideas based on that work. Interdisciplinary work, for example, requires reading selections from multiple resources, engaging in expressions of ideas, collaboration with others, and long-term processes that require more work. Learning experiences for the gifted may require more time to complete, process, discuss, and incubate than might be expected in learning experiences for typical learners.

Implementing the standards in the classroom. An implementation section has been written for each activity set in order to provide guidance to the teacher in using the activities specified in respect to time, grouping approach, the discussion mode, and the monitoring of small-group and individual project work.

Time has been specified only in respect to minimum numbers of periods needed for the implementation of the learning experiences provided. Typically, a three-part lesson would represent at least three periods, one for discussion and other activities, one for writing, and one for presentations. However, time periods may vary considerably, given classroom variables.

There is an underlying assumption of the authors that gifted students would be grouped in cluster settings within general education classrooms, pull-out settings, or in self-contained classrooms for purposes of the implementation of the CCSS-ELA work that requires differentiation. The examples could also be used in centers that cater to differentiated activities or as part of independent work for advanced learners. Regardless of the grouping pattern employed, one of the important distinctions of the examples for advanced learners is the use of advanced literature in respect to Lexile level and complexity. Thus the nature of the activity is not the only aspect of differentiation employed in the standard examples in literature. It is also the reading level of the literature selected for the examples.

Discussion modes employed in the examples favor the use of Socratic seminars that offer a deeper explication of ideas than what is typically provided in a literature circle. Discussion is also highlighted by using structured questions that employ strong emphasis on higher level thinking.

There is also an emphasis in the implementation sections of the examples on teacher monitoring of the work students are doing in the classroom. Such monitoring may take the form of moving among groups, using informal checklists, and asking clarifying questions.

Assessment. Assessment ideas for each activity set are included with rubric suggestions for teacher use. The assessment section of this book, and the earlier book, is referenced for assessment archetypes that align with the performance-based models being used in the construction of the new assessment system linked to the CCSS-ELA. Thus, examples of how informational text may be assessed are provided and include literary text analysis items, writing items, and speaking and listening rubrics. In this way, teachers may proceed to design tailored assessments for their classroom that have viability in the preparation of students for the new state assessments due out in 2014 that will replace state tests in CCSS states. It may be useful to refer to the websites of the two state assessment consortia for the new test blueprints. See http://www.smarterbalanced.org and http://www.parcconline.org.

We encourage readers to consult the assessment section on page 132 of this book for rubric ideas, the rubric chart of sample approaches (on p. 134), and references to websites that contain relevant rubrics. We also encourage readers to consult with the first NAGC book on CCSS-ELA (VanTassel-Baska, 2013) for sample assessment tools and rubrics for reading literature, writing, and speaking and listening.

Resources. Resources are provided that guide the readers to research-based materials for use in language arts classrooms. Each of the materials listed has evidence of effectiveness with gifted and advanced readers at designated grade levels. Moreover, generic resources are also included that may aid teachers in selecting appropriate texts. We have also included in the appendix sections relevant studies that have been conducted on language arts curricula for the gifted, as well as related studies that may guide any decision making concerning language arts issues of curriculum, instruction, and assessment.

Introduction to the Scope and Sequence of the Reading Literature and Informational Text Standards

In order to understand the examples that have been developed to illustrate how to differentiate the CCSS–ELA for the gifted, it is first necessary to understand the organization of the standards themselves.

Anchor Strands for English Language Arts

Each of the five areas within the CCSS–ELA standards (reading, writing, language, and speaking and listening) is headed by a strand-specific set of College and Career Readiness Anchor (CCRA) Standards that provide the foundation for the strand.

For example, the reading standards for both informational text and literature, on which this guide is focused, include 10 literacy anchor standards, which are grouped around four skill areas:

1. *Key Ideas and Details* (CCRA.R1, CCRA.R2, CCRA.R3)
2. *Craft and Structure* (CCRA.R4, CCRA.R5, CCRA.R6)
3. *Integration of Knowledge and Ideas* (CCRA.R7, CCRA.R8, CCRA.R9)
4. *Range and Level of Text Complexity* (CCRA.R10)

The anchor standards, together with the grade-specific standards, define the skills and understandings that all students must demonstrate by the end of high school (NGA & CCSSO, 2010). Note that each anchor standard number corresponds to the strand numbers within the grade-specific standards (e.g., CCRA.R1 corresponds to Strand 1 of the Literature and Informational Text Standards).

Progression of Grade-Level Reading Standards in Four Strands

The Reading for Literature and Reading for Informational Text standards, which are discussed in this text, each contain grade-level standards in 10 strand areas. The complete list of the reading literature and informational text standards, in four of the strands, is presented in the following tables. In bold type are the standards the authors selected for designing specific examples in this text. The notations in the right column of each chart delineate how the standard changes from one grade level to the next, beginning with kindergarten.

To work with the standards across grade levels, educators must understand the way they are vertically aligned. By using these tables as a reference for curriculum modeling, teachers can easily see the extent of the change in the intent of the standard as students progress through school. They also illustrate the overlap in the same standard strands at different grade levels, suggesting that there is a need to craft differentiated task demands at each grade level to address the anchor standard, which overarches each strand.

The tables also demonstrate the similarity between the reading literature and informational text standards. Very few differences other than text choices differentiate the two sets of standards. Thus, teachers may wish to correlate a given reading skill found in both sets of standards (e.g., determining theme) and identify core readings that advanced students should access that represent both literature and informational text.

Reading Literature: A Scope and Sequence of Standards by Strand

Anchor Standard in Literacy for Strand 2

Determine central ideas or themes of a text and analyze their development; summarize the key supporting details and ideas.

Grade-Specific Standards in Strand 2	Analysis of How the Standard Changes From One Grade to the Next
RL.K.2: With prompting and support, retell familiar stories, including key details.	
RL.1.2: Retell stories, including key details, and demonstrate understanding of their central message or lesson.	Removes prompting and support; adds an emphasis on understanding main idea.
RL.2.2: Recount stories, including fables and folktales from diverse cultures, and determine their central message, lesson, or moral.	Elaborates on the genre to be applied; adds the cultural diversity factor.
RL.3.2: Recount stories, including fables, folktales, and myths from diverse cultures; determine the central message, lesson, or moral and explain how it is conveyed through key details in the text.	**Adds the genre of myth; adds the explanation of how main idea is conveyed through textual details.**
RL.4.2: Determine a theme of a story, drama, or poem from details in the text; summarize the text.	Recrafts the standard to reflect the identification of theme, details that reveal it and broadened genres of story, drama, or poetry in which it is found; adds summarizing the text.
RL.5.2: Determine a theme of a story, drama, or poem from details in the text, including how characters in a story or drama respond to challenges or how the speaker in a poem reflects upon a topic; summarize the text.	**Elaborates on character response to challenge or speaker reflection in a poem.**
RL.6.2: Determine a theme or central idea of a text and how it is conveyed through particular details; provide a summary of the text distinct from personal opinions or judgments.	Emphasizes providing an objective summary of text.
RL.7.2: Determine a theme or central idea of a text and analyze its development over the course of the text; provide an objective summary of the text.	Adds an analysis of the development of the main idea over the course of the text.

Grade-Specific Standards in Strand 2	Analysis of How the Standard Changes From One Grade to the Next
RL.8.2: Determine a theme or central idea of a text and analyze its development over the course of the text, including its relationship to the characters, setting, and plot; provide an objective summary of the text.	Adds an emphasis on showing the relationship of theme to character, setting, and plot.
RL.9–10.2: Determine a theme or central idea of a text and analyze in detail its development over the course of the text, including how it emerges and is shaped and refined by specific details; provide an objective summary of the text.	Adds how an idea emerges and is shaped/refined by details.
RL.11–12.2: Determine two or more themes or central ideas of a text and analyze their development over the course of the text, including how they interact and build on one another to produce a complex account; provide an objective summary of the text.	Adds an analysis of two themes and how they interact intertextually (AP and IB level).

Anchor Strand in Literacy for Strand 3

Analyze how and why individuals, events, or ideas develop and interact over the course of a text.

Grade-Specific Standards in Strand 3	Analysis of How the Standard Changes From One Grade to the Next
RL.K.3: With prompting and support, identify characters, settings, and major events in a story..	
RL.1.3: Describe characters, settings, and major events in a story, using key details.	Goes beyond reading to ask for key details to describe character, settings and plot.
RL.2.3: Describe how characters in a story respond to major events and challenges.	Emphasizes how characters respond to events in the text.
RL.3.3: Describe characters in a story (e.g., their traits, motivations, or feelings) and explain how their actions contribute to the sequence of events	Emphasizes the role of character action as a basis for sequence of events.
RL.4.3: Describe in depth a character, setting, or event in a story or drama, drawing on specific details in the text (e.g., a character's thoughts, words, or actions).	Focuses on depth of character analysis.

Grade-Specific Standards in Strand 3	Analysis of How the Standard Changes From One Grade to the Next
RL.5.3: Compare and contrast two or more characters, settings, or events in a story or drama, drawing on specific details in the text (e.g., how characters interact).	Calls for comparative analysis of characters, settings, or events.
RL.6.3: Describe how a particular story's or drama's plot unfolds in a series of episodes as well as how the characters respond or change as the plot moves toward a resolution.	Focuses on plot structure development.
RL.7.3: Analyze how particular elements of a story or drama interact (e.g., how setting shapes the characters or plot).	Focuses on the interaction of literary elements.
RL.8.3: Analyze how particular lines of dialogue or incidents in a story or drama propel the action, reveal aspects of a character, or provoke a decision.	Focuses on dialogue or incidents that move the plot forward.
RL.9–10.3: Analyze how complex characters (e.g., those with multiple or conflicting motivations) develop over the course of a text, interact with other characters, and advance the plot or develop the theme.	Emphasizes the complexity of characters who develop, interact and advance the plot.
RL.11–12.3: Analyze the impact of the author's choices regarding how to develop and relate elements of a story or drama (e.g., where a story is set, how the action is ordered, how the characters are introduced and developed).	Emphasizes author's choices for story development.

Anchor Strand in Literacy for Strand 4

Interpret words and phrases as they are used in a text, including determining technical, connotative, and figurative meanings, and analyze how specific word choices shape meaning or tone.

Grade-Specific Standards in Strand 4	Analysis of How the Standard Changes From One Grade to the Next
RL.K.4: Ask and answer questions about unknown words in a text..	

Grade-Specific Standards in Strand 4	Analysis of How the Standard Changes From One Grade to the Next
RL.1.4: Identify words and phrases in stories or poems that suggest feelings or appeal to the senses.	Focuses on vocabulary used to provoke feelings.
RL.2.4: Describe how words and phrases (e.g., regular beats, alliteration, rhymes, repeated lines) supply rhythm and meaning in a story, poem, or song.	Focuses on literary devices as a tool to create meaning.
RL.3.4: Determine the meaning of words and phrases as they are used in a text, distinguishing literal from nonliteral language.	**Focuses on the distinction of literal and nonliteral language.**
RL.4.4: Determine the meaning of words and phrases as they are used in a text, including those that allude to significant characters found in mythology (e.g., Herculean).	Same as RL.3.4.
RL.5.4: Determine the meaning of words and phrases as they are used in a text, including figurative language such as metaphors and similes.	**Focuses on word meanings, including figurative language defined as similes and metaphors.**
RL.6.4: Determine the meaning of words and phrases as they are used in a text, including figurative and connotative meanings; analyze the impact of a specific word choice on meaning and tone.	Adds the term "connotative meanings"; adds a focus on word choice and analysis on tone and meaning.
RL.7.4: Determine the meaning of words and phrases as they are used in a text, including figurative and connotative meanings; analyze the impact of rhymes and other repetitions of sounds (e.g., alliteration) on a specific verse or stanza of a poem or section of a story or drama.	Emphasizes rhyme and repetition of sounds for analysis of impact of words on specific text sections.
RL.8.4: Determine the meaning of words and phrases as they are used in a text, including figurative and connotative meanings; analyze the impact of specific word choices on meaning and tone, including analogies or allusions to other texts.	**Emphasizes analogies and allusions to other texts for analysis of word choices.**

Grade-Specific Standards in Strand 4	Analysis of How the Standard Changes From One Grade to the Next
RL.9–10.4: Determine the meaning of words and phrases as they are used in the text, including figurative and connotative meanings; analyze the cumulative impact of specific word choices on meaning and tone (e.g., how the language evokes a sense of time and place; how it sets a formal or informal tone).	Adds an emphasis on cumulative impact of word choices.
RL.11–12.4: Determine the meaning of words and phrases as they are used in the text, including figurative and connotative meanings; analyze the impact of specific word choices on meaning and tone, including words with multiple meanings or language that is particularly fresh, engaging, or beautiful. (Include Shakespeare as well as other authors.)	Adds an emphasis on word choices that have layered meanings and those that are attractive.

Anchor Strand in Literacy for Strand 9

Analyze how two or more texts address similar themes or topics in order to build knowledge or to compare the approaches the authors take.

Grade-Specific Standards in Strand 9	Analysis of How the Standard Changes From One Grade to the Next
RL.K.9: With prompting and support, compare and contrast the adventures and experiences of characters in familiar stories.	
RL.1.9: Compare and contrast the adventures and experiences of characters in stories.	Removes prompting and support and familiar stories.
RL.2.9: Compare and contrast two or more versions of the same story (e.g., Cinderella stories) by different authors or from different cultures.	Adds comparative analysis of two story versions from different authors or cultures.

Grade-Specific Standards in Strand 9	Analysis of How the Standard Changes From One Grade to the Next
RL.3.9: Compare and contrast the themes, settings, and plots of stories written by the same author about the same or similar characters (e.g., in books from a series).	**Adds comparative analysis of theme, setting, and plot of stories by same author with similar characters.**
RL.4.9: Compare and contrast the treatment of similar themes and topics (e.g., opposition of good and evil) and patterns of events (e.g., the quest) in stories, myths, and traditional literature from different cultures.	Adds comparative analysis of themes and patterns in various genres across cultures.
RL.5.9: Compare and contrast stories in the same genre (e.g., mysteries and adventure stories) on their approaches to similar themes and topics.	**Changes the comparative analysis of theme and topic to within genre works.**
RL.6.9: Compare and contrast texts in different forms or genres (e.g., stories and poems; historical novels and fantasy stories) in terms of their approaches to similar themes and topics.	Very close to RL.4.9.
RL.7.9: Compare and contrast a fictional portrayal of a time, place, or character and a historical account of the same period as a means of understanding how authors of fiction use or alter history.	Adds comparative analysis of a fictional account of history with other authentic sources.
RL.8.9: Analyze how a modern work of fiction draws on themes, patterns of events, or character types from myths, traditional stories, or religious works such as the Bible, including describing how the material is rendered new.	**Analyzes the continuity of literary themes, patterns of events, and archetypes across time and culture.**
RL.9–10.9: Analyze how an author draws on and transforms source material in a specific work (e.g., how Shakespeare treats a theme or topic from Ovid or the Bible or how a later author draws on a play by Shakespeare).	**Analyzes how an author transforms ancient source material.**

Grade-Specific Standards in Strand 9	Analysis of How the Standard Changes From One Grade to the Next
RL.11–12.9: Demonstrate knowledge of eighteenth-, nineteenth- and early-twentieth-century foundational works of American literature, including how two or more texts from the same period treat similar themes or topics.	Adds comparative analysis of a theme in two or more texts in American literature, selected from 18th–20th century options. (AP-IB Level)

Reading Informational Text: A Scope and Sequence of Standards by Strand

Anchor Standard in Literacy for Strand 2

Determine central ideas or themes of a text and analyze their development; summarize the key supporting details and ideas.

Grade-Specific Standards in Strand 2	Analysis of How the Standard Changes From One Grade to the Next
RI.K.2: With prompting and support, identify the main topic and retell key details of a text.	
RI.1.2: Identify the main topic and retell key details of a text.	Changes from support to independent work.
RI.2.2: Identify the main topic of a multi-paragraph text as well as the focus of specific paragraphs within the text.	Focus changes to multiparagraph text and topical emphasis within selected paragraphs.
RI.3.2: Determine the main idea of a text; recount the key details and explain how they support the main idea.	**Changes from topic to main idea of text and how details support that idea.**
RI.4.2: Determine the main idea of a text and explain how it is supported by key details; summarize the text.	Adds summarization of text.
RI.5.2: Determine two or more main ideas of a text and explain how they are supported by key details; summarize the text.	**Adds two or more main ideas.**
RI.6.2: Determine a central idea of a text and how it is conveyed through particular details; provide a summary of the text distinct from personal opinions or judgments.	Adds objective summary of text.

Grade-Specific Standards in Strand 2	Analysis of How the Standard Changes From One Grade to the Next
RI.7.2: Determine two or more central ideas in a text and analyze their development over the course of the text; provide an objective summary of the text.	Adds multiple main ideas and analysis of their development.
RI.8.2: Determine a central idea of a text and analyze its development over the course of the text, including its relationship to supporting ideas; provide an objective summary of the text.	**Adds relationship of main idea to supporting ideas.**
RI.9–10.2: Determine a central idea of a text and analyze its development over the course of the text, including how it emerges and is shaped and refined by specific details; provide an objective summary of the text.	**Adds how ideas emerge and are shaped by details.**
RI.11–12.2: Determine two or more central ideas of a text and analyze their development over the course of the text, including how they interact and build on one another to provide a complex analysis; provide an objective summary of the text.	Adds how ideas in a text interact and build on each other to provide a complex analysis.

Anchor Strand in Literacy for Strand 3

Analyze how and why individuals, events, or ideas develop and interact over the course of a text.

Grade-Specific Standards in Strand 3	Analysis of How the Standard Changes from One Grade to the Next
RI.K.3: With prompting and support, describe the connection between two individuals, events, ideas, or pieces of information in a text.	
RI.1.3: Describe the connection between two individuals, events, ideas, or pieces of information in a text.	Changes from support to independent work.
RI.2.3: Describe the connection between a series of historical events, scientific ideas or concepts, or steps in technical procedures in a text.	Becomes more specific in respect to relationship between historical events, scientific ideas, or steps in technical procedures.

Grade-Specific Standards in Strand 3	Analysis of How the Standard Changes from One Grade to the Next
RI.3.3: Describe the relationship between a series of historical events, scientific ideas or concepts, or steps in technical procedures in a text, using language that pertains to time, sequence, and cause/effect.	**Adds language related to time, sequence, and cause and effect.**
RI.4.3: Explain events, procedures, ideas, or concepts in a historical, scientific, or technical text, including what happened and why, based on specific information in the text.	Adds an emphasis on describing what happened and why, based on text info.
RI.5.3: Explain the relationships or interactions between two or more individuals, events, ideas, or concepts in a historical, scientific, or technical text based on specific information in the text.	**Adds the need to explain the relationships or interactions between individuals, events, or ideas.**
RI.6.3: Analyze in detail how a key individual, event, or idea is introduced, illustrated, and elaborated in a text (e.g., through examples or anecdotes).	Emphasizes analysis of how ideas are introduced, illustrated, and elaborated in text.
RI.7.3: Analyze the interactions between individuals, events, and ideas in a text (e.g., how ideas influence individuals or events, or how individuals influence ideas or events).	Adds the dimension of influence of people on events and vice versa.
RI.8.3: Analyze how a text makes connections among and distinctions between individuals, ideas, or events (e.g., through comparisons, analogies, or categories).	**Focuses on connections and distinctions among individuals, events, and ideas in text.**
RI.9–10.3: Analyze how the author unfolds an analysis or series of ideas or events, including the order in which the points are made, how they are introduced and developed, and the connections that are drawn between them.	**Focuses on author intent in sequencing, development, and connections made in an analysis of people, events or ideas.**
RI.11–12.3: Analyze a complex set of ideas or sequence of events and explain how specific individuals, ideas, or events interact and develop over the course of the text.	Focuses on analysis of ideas or sequence of events and explains how ideas interact and develop through the text.

Anchor Strand in Literacy for Strand 4

Interpret words and phrases as they are used in a text, including determining technical, connotative, and figurative meanings, and analyze how specific word choices shape meaning or tone.

Grade-Specific Standards in Strand 4	Analysis of How the Standard Changes From One Grade to the Next
RI.K.4: With prompting and support, ask and answer questions about unknown words in a text.	
RI.1.4: Ask and answer questions to help determine or clarify the meaning of words and phrases in a text.	Changes from support to independent work.
RI.2.4: Determine the meaning of words and phrases in a text relevant to a *grade 2 topic or subject area.*	Adds grade 2 topic or subject found in text.
RI.3.4: Determine the meaning of general academic and domain-specific words and phrases in a text relevant to a *grade 3 topic or subject area.*	**Adds meaning of academic words and phrases found in text on grade 3 topic or subject.**
RI.4.4: Determine the meaning of general academic and domain-specific words or phrases in a text relevant to a *grade 4 topic or subject area.*	Changes to grade 4 topics.
RI.5.4: Determine the meaning of general academic and domain-specific words and phrases in a text relevant to a *grade 5 topic or subject area.*	**Changes to grade 5 topics.**
RI.6.4: Determine the meaning of words and phrases as they are used in a text, including figurative, connotative, and technical meanings.	Focuses on figurative, connotative, and technical meanings.
RI.7.4: Determine the meaning of words and phrases as they are used in a text, including figurative, connotative, and technical meanings; analyze the impact of a specific word.	Adds the analysis of word impact.
RI.8.4: Determine the meaning of words and phrases as they are used in a text, including figurative, connotative, and technical meanings; analyze the impact of specific word choices on meaning and tone, including analogies or allusions to other texts.	**Adds the analysis of word choices on meaning and tone (including analogies or allusions).**

Grade-Specific Standards in Strand 4	Analysis of How the Standard Changes From One Grade to the Next
RI.9–10.4: Determine the meaning of words and phrases as they are used in a text, including figurative, connotative, and technical meanings; analyze the cumulative impact of specific word choices on meaning and tone (e.g., how the language of a court opinion differs from that of a newspaper).	Adds *cumulative* impact of word choices.
RI.11–12.4: Determine the meaning of words and phrases as they are used in a text, including figurative, connotative, and technical meanings; analyze how an author uses and refines the meaning of a key term or terms over the course of a text (e.g., how Madison defines faction in Federalist No. 10).	Adds an analysis of author use and refinement of meaning of terms over the course of a text.

Anchor Strand in Literacy for Strand 9

Analyze how two or more texts address similar themes or topics in order to build knowledge or to compare the approaches the authors take.

Grade-Specific Standards in Strand 9	Analysis of How the Standard Changes From One Grade to the Next
RI.K.9: With prompting and support, identify basic similarities in and differences between two texts on the same topic (e.g., in illustrations, descriptions, or procedures).	
RI.1.9: Identify basic similarities in and differences between two texts on the same topic (e.g., in illustrations, descriptions, or procedures).	Changes from support to independent work.
RI.2.9: Compare and contrast the most important points presented by two texts on the same topic.	Focuses on comparative analysis of two texts.
RI.3.9: Compare and contrast the most important points and key details presented in two texts on the same topic.	**Adds analysis of key details**

Grade-Specific Standards in Strand 9	Analysis of How the Standard Changes From One Grade to the Next
RI.4.9: Integrate information from two texts on the same topic in order to write or speak about the subject knowledgeably.	Focuses on synthesis of information from two texts for the purpose of writing or speaking.
RI.5.9: Integrate information from several texts on the same topic in order to write or speak about the subject knowledgeably.	**Adds multiple texts.**
RI.6.9: Compare and contrast one author's presentation of events with that of another (e.g., a memoir written by and a biography on the same person).	Analyzes the same events presented by two authors.
RI.7.9: Analyze how two or more authors writing about the same topic shape their presentations of key information by emphasizing different evidence or advancing different interpretations of facts.	Adds the need to examine differences in evidence presented and differing interpretation of facts.
RI.8.9: Analyze a case in which two or more texts provide conflicting information on the same topic and identify where the texts disagree on matters of fact or interpretation.	**Analyzes textual disagreement on fact and interpretation.**
RI.9–10.9: Analyze seminal U.S. documents of historical and literary significance (e.g., Washington's Farewell Address, the Gettysburg Address, Roosevelt's Four Freedoms speech, King's "Letter from Birmingham Jail"), including how they address related themes and concepts.	**Focuses on the analysis of seminal U.S. documents for related themes and concepts.**
RI.11–12.9: Analyze seventeenth-, eighteenth-, and nineteenth-century foundational U.S. documents of historical and literary significance (including The Declaration of Independence, the Preamble to the Constitution, the Bill of Rights, and Lincoln's Second Inaugural Address) for their themes, purposes, and rhetorical features.	Emphasizes analysis of 17th–19th century U.S. documents for theme, purposes, and rhetoric.

Reading Literature Examples

The examples that follow for reading literature have been selected to demonstrate what a typical learner might be asked to do to address a given standard and then how one might choose to differentiate a reading literature task for advanced or gifted learners. In most cases, the advanced learner's task demands integrated opportunities for addressing multiple standards in writing and speaking and listening, in addition to reading literature. The specific standards used to craft the activity in writing and speaking and listening are included for easy reference. Each example also addresses specific approaches employed to differentiate the advanced learner activity. Usually, two or more approaches have been applied that include the use of higher Lexile-level text (typically two grade levels above), complexity, depth, and creativity. Each example also offers the teacher suggestions for implementation such as grouping, minimum time frames needed, and use of discussion models. Assessment considerations are also noted with references to the first NAGC CCSS-ELA book (VanTassel-Baska, 2013) and the assessment section in this volume for specific rubrics.

Users of this guide are encouraged to visit sites that provide access to recommended literary materials. Although the authors use specific examples from the texts cited, we encourage the reader to view these as examples only, not necessarily as recommended curriculum for use in classrooms. Any of the examples cited should be reviewed by teachers for appropriateness for their students and context.

Sample Differentiated Learning Experiences in Reading Literature Standards

RL Standard 2 Grade 3

Connections to Writing and Speaking/Listening

CCSS.ELA-Literacy Writing.3.1: Write opinion pieces on topics or texts supporting a point of view with reasons.

CCSS.ELA-Literacy Speaking/Listening.3.1: Engage effectively in a range of collaborative discussions (one-on-one, in groups, and teacher-led) with diverse partners on grade 3 topics and texts, building on others' ideas and expressing their own clearly.

Implementation Considerations

This series of activities will take two class periods. Part I should be done with the whole group. Parts II and III should be done individually. Discussion approach to the fable should use guiding questions and be led by the teacher. Monitoring of the creation of fables should be done during the first class session, with the teacher providing comments to individual students as she rotates throughout the classroom. If possible, all the fables should be available online for inclusion in a class booklet. If needed, students should finish the product at home and come prepared to share the next day.

Differentiation Considerations

This learning experience was differentiated using:
- more advanced and in-depth questions,
- more complex thought processes required (synthesis),
- product demands that call for greater creativity and effort, and
- use of abstract themes as a basis for application.

Assessment Considerations

The assessment approach may entail observation of student discussion and product assessment of fable and accompanying illustration.

RL Standard 2 Grade 3

Grade and Standard	Typical Learners	Advanced Learners
Grade 3 RL.3.2: Recount stories, including fables, folktales, and myths from diverse cultures; determine the central message, lesson, or moral and explain how it is conveyed through key details in the text.	**Part I** Ask students to read Aesop's fable *The Tortoise and the Hare* (Daily, 2007). Then ask students the following questions about the fable: 1. What are the characteristics of the tortoise and the hare? Create a comparison chart that uses adjectives to describe how they are different. What words does Aesop use that convey how the two animals are different from each other? 2. What idea do you take from the fable about which qualities matter in life? What evidence supports your opinion about this? 3. Why is the ending of the fable unexpected? 4. Can you think of a real-life example of a race being won in a similar manner? Share with the class. **Part II** Have students draw a picture that illustrates the most important scene from the fable, title it appropriately, and describe why they chose this depiction. **Part III** Ask students to share the illustrations created.	**Part I** Ask students to read Aesop's fable *The Tortoise and the Hare* (Daily, 2007) . Then ask students the following questions about the fable: 1. What are the characteristics of the tortoise and the hare? Create a comparison chart that uses adjectives to describe how they are different. What words does Aesop use that convey how the two animals are different from each other? 2. What idea do you take from the fable about which qualities matter in life? What evidence supports your opinion about this? 3. Why is the ending of the fable unexpected? 4. How effective is the fable in helping you understand the importance of the quality of persistence? 5. Can you think of a real-life example of a race being won in a similar manner? Share with the class. **Part II: Writing** Ask students to create a fable that has a similar moral or lesson, using other animals to illustrate the point. Be sure to provide a clear sequence of action. Draw a picture that illustrates a scene from the fable and title it appropriately. **Part III: Speaking/Listening** Have students share the fables and illustrations created. Ask students to provide an artist's statement about their fable and picture that explores why they chose the animals they did, why they organized their story in the sequence they did, and why they titled their picture the way they did.

RL Standard 2 Grade 5

Connections to Writing and Speaking/Listening

CCSS.ELA-Literacy.Writing.5.7: Conduct short research projects that use several sources to build knowledge through investigation of different aspects of a topic.

CCSS.ELA-Literacy.Speaking/Listening.5.5: Include multimedia components (e.g., graphics, sound) and visual displays in presentations when appropriate to enhance the development of main ideas or themes.

Implementation Considerations

This series of activities will take at least three periods to complete. Students may work in small groups of four to five to do Part I. Students may work in dyads (or pairs) to complete Part II. Students will independently carry out Part III of the activity. Discussion will be guided by the questions and the tasks assigned. Project work will be monitored by teachers through rotation among groups, questioning individual students about progress, and asking for formative work samples as appropriate.

Differentiation Considerations

This learning experience was differentiated using:
- greater complexity,
- in-depth exploration of myth in two cultures,
- use of abstract ideas as a basis for application, and
- use of creative product assignment.

Assessment Considerations

This task demand may be assessed by the use of a rubric to judge the research papers, using the criteria of completeness, choice of resources, argument, and quality of writing. Another rubric may be used to judge the shield presentation, using the criteria of aptness of the symbol selected, articulation of rationale, and overall presentation.

RL Standard 2 Grade 5

Grade and Standard	Typical Learners	Advanced Learners
Grade 5 RL.5.2: Determine a theme of a story, drama, or poem from details in the text, including how characters in a story or drama respond to challenges or how the speaker in a poem reflects upon a topic; summarize the text.	Ask students to prepare a set of shields that depict important symbols for three gods and/or goddesses from one ancient civilization about which you have read online. Have them create a rationale for choosing the symbols they have selected. If they were to use one word to describe your deity, what would it be and why? Ask three students to present their work and display all as part of a class exhibit.	**Part I** Ask students to read the entry from *Bulfinch's Mythology* (Bulfinch, 2008) on the deities of Hindu mythology. Now have them read about Greek gods and goddesses from the same source material. Ask the following questions about the readings and ask students to complete the chart (see below for chart headers): 1. What challenges did each set of gods and goddesses face? 2. How did they respond to those challenges? 3. Summarize your understanding of the connections between Hindu and Greek mythology as seen in the depiction of deities. Hand out chart (Row headers: God/Goddess, Indian, Greek, Challenge, Response). **Part II: Writing** Ask students to construct a guide to world mythology that highlights a common type of deity in at least three different cultures. Have them write a 2–3-page research paper describing the similarities and differences of these deities as they are depicted in myth. What do they think accounts for the connections across cultures? Ask students to defend their position in their final section of the research paper. **Part III: Speaking/Listening** Ask students to prepare a set of shields that depict important symbols for three gods and/or goddesses from one ancient civilization. Have them create a rationale for choosing the symbols they have selected. If they were to use one word to describe your deity, what would it be and why? Ask three students to present their work and display all as part of a class exhibit.

RL Standard 2 Grade 8

Connections to Writing and Speaking/Listening

CCSS.ELA-Literacy.Writing.8.1: Write arguments to support claims with clear reasons and relevant evidence.

CCSS.ELA-Literacy.Speaking/Listening.8.4: Engage effectively in a range of collaborative discussions (one-on-one, in groups, and teacher-led) with diverse partners on grade 8 topics, texts, and issues, building on others' ideas and expressing their own clearly.

Implementation Considerations

This activity will require at least four periods to complete, two for the debate. Preparation for the debate will occur outside of class time and be based on the in-class writing assignment. Selected individuals will be called on to contribute to the discussion in Parts I and II. The teacher will provide the format outline for the debate along with the hamburger model for persuasive writing. Both can be laminated and put up in the room as well.

Differentiation Considerations

This learning experience was differentiated using:
- greater complexity,
- more in-depth exploration of theme and argument, and
- greater use of critical and creative thinking.

Assessment Considerations

The assessments used for this task demand would include:
- a teacher and self-assessment for the paragraphs on accuracy and commentary of the three key dimensions of theme, character, and plot;
- a teacher and self-assessment of the persuasive writing assignment; and

- an assessment of the debate presentation, focusing on the criteria of evidence of preparation, use of logical argument, clarity, and effectiveness of presentation.

RL Standard 2 Grade 8

Grade and Standard	Typical Learners	Advanced Learners
Grade 8 RL.8.2: Determine a theme or central idea of a text and analyze its development over the course of the text, including its relationship to the characters, setting, and plot; provide an objective summary of the text.	Ask students to read about Arthur, legendary king of Britain, in the section entitled "Arthur Is Chosen King" from *Le Morte D'Arthur* (Malory, 1485/1970). Then have them do the following: 1. Summarize the text in a paragraph. Include the central idea, how characters contribute to that idea, the setting of the text, and the action that takes place. 2. Use a visualizer to project three summary paragraphs of different students. Discuss the ideas shared, the characterizations provided, and the settings and plot structures articulated. 3. Using the assessment provided, rate the paragraphs on the accuracy and commentary of the three key dimensions of theme, character, and plot.	**Part I** Ask students to read about Arthur, legendary king of Britain, in the section entitled "Arthur Is Chosen King" from *Le Morte D'Arthur* (Malory, 1485/1970). Then have them do the following: 1. Summarize the text read in a paragraph. Include the central idea, how characters contribute to that idea, the setting of the text, and the action that takes place. 2. Use a visualizer to project three summary paragraphs of different students. Discuss the ideas shared, the characterizations provided, and the settings and plot structures articulated. 3. Using the assessment provided, rate the paragraphs on the accuracy and commentary of the three key dimensions of theme, character, and plot. **Part II: Writing** Ask students to address the following prompt for an in-class 30-minute persuasive writing exercise (Students will use the hamburger model as the guide for their work): *Rulers should be selected based on their human qualities rather than their deeds and exploits.* Discuss the position taken by about six students and ask them to share reasons for their perspective. Ask students to apply a persuasive writing rubric to their own writing piece and revise based on their assessment. Turn in their writing for teacher assessment, using the same rubric. **Part III: Speaking/Listening** Stage a debate that features teams of four students, providing their resolution on the issue, affirmative and negative rebuttals, and a recap of the key points. The total presentation time for each group should not exceed 20 minutes.

RL Standard 2 Grades 9–10

Connections to Writing and Speaking/Listening

CCSS.ELA-Literacy.Writing.9–10.3: Write narratives to develop real or imagined experiences or events using effective technique, well-chosen details, and well-structured event sequences.

CCSS.ELA-Literacy.Speaking/Listening.9–10.5: Make strategic use of digital media (e.g., textual, graphical, audio, visual, and interactive elements) in presentations to enhance understanding of and add interest to findings, reasoning, and evidence.

Implementation Considerations

This activity set will take at least three periods and homework time to complete. Teachers should hold a full-group discussion of the story, using the Socratic seminar method (see *The Teaching Channel* resource on page 153). Students should model the style of William Carlos Williams as a basis for their poems. Additional readings by Lawrence and the web on his style should be completed outside of class. Presentations should be done in class.

Differentiation Considerations

This learning experience was differentiated using:
- choice of writer and literature,
- more complexity,
- greater depth of exploration of literary elements, and
- delineation of products.

Assessment Considerations

The assessment of these tasks may include a product assessment for the poem created, an observation tool for the discussions held (especially the Socratic seminar), and a presentation assessment form and rubric.

RL Standard 2 Grades 9–10

Grade and Standard	Typical Learners	Advanced Learners
Grade 9–10 RL.9–10.2: Determine a theme or central idea of a text and analyze in detail its development over the course of the text, including how it emerges and is shaped and refined by specific details; provide an objective summary of the text.	**Part I** Have students read the short story *The Lottery* by Shirley Jackson (1949/2005) before coming to class. In pairs, ask them to complete a literature web, noting key words, themes, feelings, images and symbols, and structure of the story. **Part II** Ask students to write a persuasive essay in 30 minutes on the following prompt: *Should punishment be carried out in public?* Students should remember to create an opening and closing paragraph and three paragraphs that each describe a reason they are making their assertions.	**Part I** Ask students to read the D. H. Lawrence (1926/2007) short story *The Rocking Horse Winner* before coming to class and complete a literature web on it, commenting on key words, feelings, ideas, symbols, and the structure of the story. Using their webs as the basis, discuss the following questions: 1. What is the key action sequence in the story? 2. What are the qualities that Hester reveals about herself in the story? How do these qualities unfold over time? 3. What evidence is there in the story that it will end the way it does? 4. What ideas are central to understanding the story? How does the theme develop over the course of the story? 5. If you were to change the title, what would it be? Why do you think Lawrence chose this title? **Part II: Writing** Ask students to summarize the meaning of the rocking horse in the story. What does it symbolize? Have them create a poem à la William Carlos Williams' (1985) "The Red Wheelbarrow" about a rocking horse. The students will share the poems in class. **Part III: Speaking/Listening** Have students read two other short stories by D. H. Lawrence; create and present a multimedia presentation that summarizes the themes he uses, the plot structures, the settings, and the characterizations he depicts. What other features of style can they identify in Lawrence? The students will share their reactions to his style.

RL Standard 3 Grade 3

Connections to Writing and Speaking/Listening

CCSS.ELA-Literacy.Writing.3.3: Write narratives to develop real or imagined experiences or events using effective technique, descriptive details, and clear event sequences.

CCSS.ELA-Literacy.Speaking/Listening.5.1: Engage effectively in a range of collaborative discussions (one-on-one, in groups, and teacher-led) with diverse partners on grade 5 topics and texts, building on others' ideas and expressing their own clearly.

Implementation Considerations

For Part I prereading (questions 1–3), students will consider the material independently. After reading the text, the teacher will facilitate a whole-class discussion of the "Questions for Discussion."

Part II may be assigned as homework or as an individual in-class writing assignment. Part III should be done in small groups.

The teacher will facilitate prereading and postreading discussion and will monitor in-class writing (if not completed for homework) and small-group response groups. The teacher should provide comments to individual students while they write as she rotates throughout the classroom. If possible, all the final products developed after Part III should be available online for inclusion in a class booklet.

Differentiation Considerations

This learning experience was differentiated using:
- reflections about complex issues,
- creation of original stories,
- development of stories through response groups,

- product development and presentation for an authentic audience,
- infusion of multiple language arts standards,
- out-of-level objective (above level), and
- evaluation of classmates' stories.

Assessment Considerations

The in-class writing assignment will be assessed using a narrative rubric (see Kansas Department of Education, n.d., for an example). Students may also reflect on their contributions to the writing process in response groups.

RL Standard 3 Grade 3

Grade and Standard	Typical Learners	Advanced Learners
Grade 3 Standard RL.3.3: Describe characters in a story (e.g., their traits, motivations, or feelings) and explain how their actions contribute to the sequence of events.	**Part I** Students will read *Dr. DeSoto* (Steig, 1982). **Postreading Questions for Discussion** Discuss with students the characters of Dr. DeSoto and his wife: 1. What traits and motivations do they possess? 2. How does the wolf bring out their traits? 3. To what extent do their traits save their lives in this story? **Part II: Writing** Have students create a story about animals that demonstrates how problem solving can overcome difficult obstacles.	**Part I** **Prereading Questions for Discussion** 1. Have you ever wished you were someone else? 2. Have you ever wished you were invisible? 3. Have you ever wished for something and received it, but then later regretted receiving this wish? 4. In pairs, describe your recollection of one of these experiences. Read *Sylvester and the Magic Pebble* (Steig, 1987). **Questions for Discussion** 1. What were the emotions Sylvester experienced? Recall specific places in the story to illustrate your examples. 2. How did Sylvester's wish change the direction of the story? 3. What might have happened if Sylvester's wish had not been granted? **Part II: Writing** Have students create a story in which a character makes a wish and describe how the granting of the wish changes the events in the story. **Part III: Speaking/Listening** In writing response groups, students will read each story aloud and offer feedback to the writer about the development of the story. Students should be guided to listen and evaluate the story, noting strengths and areas for continued development in the stories of classmates following the reading workshop model. Students will continue to revise and refine this story and others during regular writing workshops.

RL Standard 3 Grade 5

Connections to Writing and Speaking/Listening

CCSS.ELA-Literacy.Writing.5.3: Write narratives to develop real or imagined experiences or events using effective technique, descriptive details, and clear event sequences.

CCSS.ELA-Literacy.Speaking/Listening.7.4: Present claims and findings, emphasizing salient points in a focused, coherent manner with pertinent descriptions, facts, details, and examples; use appropriate eye contact, adequate volume, and clear pronunciation.

CCSS.ELA-Literacy.Speaking/Listening.7.5: Include multimedia components and visual displays in presentations to clarify claims and findings and emphasize salient points.

CCSS.ELA-Literacy.Writing.7.7: Conduct short research projects to answer a question, drawing on several sources and generating additional related, focused questions for further research and investigation.

Implementation Considerations

Students will independently read the text prior to the class discussion. The teacher will facilitate whole-group discussion of the questions. Students will present findings from research (Part II) to the whole class.

Differentiation Considerations

This learning experience was differentiated using:
- abstract thinking about the human condition;
- development of a well-supported persuasive argument in an essay;
- product development and presentation for an authentic audience;
- consideration of literary devices;
- infusion of multiple language arts standards;

- interdisciplinary research;
- out-of-level objective (above level);
- choice provided in selection of topic for reporting to classmates;
- evaluation of trends and illustration through technology; and
- communication using images generated via technology.

Assessment Considerations

The in-class writing assignment will be assessed using the persuasive writing model rubric. The research presentation assignment will be assessed using an oral presentation rubric (ReadWriteThink, 2010). The quality of the research process as well as the elements of the presentation design may be assessed.

RL Standard 3 Grade 5

Grade and Standard	Typical Learners	Advanced Learners
Grade 5 Standard RL.5.3: Compare and contrast two or more characters, settings, or events in a story or drama, drawing on specific details in the text (e.g., how characters interact).	**Part I** Students will read *Gift of the Magi* (Henry, 1906/2008). **Discussion** 1. Who are the main characters in this story? 2. How do these characters interact with each other in this story? Based on these interactions, how would you describe their relationship? 3. What is the author's purpose in telling this story? **Part II: Writing** Ask students to develop an alternate reporting of this story that illustrates how the story would be changed if the story was told from the point of view of one of the characters.	**Part I** Students will read *Gift of the Magi* (Henry, 1906/2008). **Prereading Writing** Have students describe gift giving and receiving and indicate their view on the giver and receiver. Students will develop a persuasive essay describing a few main points to support your belief. **Discussion** 1. How would you describe Della's feelings for Jim? Jim's feelings for Della? 2. How would you describe their relationship based on your knowledge of them before they come together at the end of the story? 3. How did each character respond to the gifts? 4. What assumptions does each character make about the other? 5. How did the author maintain suspense about the plot in this story? 6. How would the story have been different if told from one character's point of view? 7. What is the guiding message this author wished to convey by telling this story? 8. In what ways are these characters "foolish"? 9. What are the symbols in this story, and what do these represent? 10. How is irony embedded in this story, and what is its effect on the ending? *continued*

RL Standard 3 Grade 5, *continued*

Grade and Standard	Typical Learners	Advanced Learners
		Part II: Writing Ask students to research the spending habits of Americans around recent holidays and compare these habits to those of other cultures over the last 5 years. Students will select an aspect of spending to consider and report to classmates: • U.S. spending trends compared to other countries, • types of holiday spending, • spending habits of men, or • spending habits of women. **Part III: Speaking/Listening** Ask students to develop a presentation to the class and provide information about one aspect of these habits to share with classmates. They will evaluate the trends in spending or habits and illustrate using graphic presentation software.

RL Standard 3 Grade 8

Connections to Writing and Speaking/Listening

CCSS.ELA-Literacy.Speaking/Listening.8.1: Engage effectively in a range of collaborative discussions (one-on-one, in groups, and teacher-led) with diverse partners on grade 8 topics, texts, and issues, building on others' ideas and expressing their own clearly.

CCSS.ELA-Literacy.Writing.8.3: Write narratives to develop real or imagined experiences or events using effective technique, relevant descriptive details, and well-structured event sequences.

CCSS.ELA-Literacy.Writing.9–10.7: Conduct short as well as more sustained research projects to answer a question (including a self-generated question) or solve a problem; narrow or broaden the inquiry when appropriate; synthesize multiple sources on the subject, demonstrating understanding of the subject under investigation.

CCSS.ELA-Literacy.Writing.9–10.2: Write informative/explanatory texts to examine and convey complex ideas, concepts, and information clearly and accurately through the effective selection, organization, and analysis of content.

Implementation Considerations

The teacher will first organize students into small groups for the initial prereading discussion and then convene the class as a large group to recap findings from each group. Students will independently read the text. Then the teacher will facilitate a whole-group discussion of the postreading questions.

Students will write a paper, comparing and contrasting their personal definitions of beauty with the culture selected. Teachers may opt to engage students in small-group or large-group conversations about the findings of their cultural research.

Differentiation Considerations

This learning experience was differentiated using:
- abstract thinking about beauty as a cultural construct;
- presentation for an authentic audience about an age-appropriate topic;
- infusion of multiple language arts standards (e.g., reading, writing, speaking and listening);
- interdisciplinary research about cultural beliefs related to beauty;
- out-of-level objective (above level);
- choice provided in selection of research area; and
- research skill development.

Assessment Considerations

The expository writing assignment may be scored using the Middle and High School Writing Rubric (Great Books Foundation, n.d.c). The research presentation assignment will be assessed using an oral presentation rubric (ReadWriteThink, 2010).

RL Standard 3 Grade 8

Grade and Standard	Typical Learners	Advanced Learners
Grade 8 Standard RL.8.3: Analyze how particular lines of dialogue or incidents in a story or drama propel the action, reveal aspects of a character, or provoke a decision.	**Part I** **Prereading Discussion** 1. Thinking back on your education thus far, identify your favorite teacher(s). 2. Explain why this individual(s) is your favorite. 3. What are the commonalities of the teachers? 4. What sets that/those teacher(s) apart? Read *Bad Boy: A Memoir* (Myers, 2001). **Part II: Writing** Ask students to write a short narrative detailing the experience they had with their favorite teachers. Consider the following questions in developing the narrative: 1. What quality did this teacher have that proved to be so effectual? 2. Is there a commonality between what you have deemed an excellent teacher and what your peers have determined makes for an outstanding teacher? 3. What advice, from your experience, do you think would be helpful for a new teacher to consider or hear? *continued*	**Part I** **Prereading Discussion** 1. What is beauty? 2. How is beauty different from ugliness? 3. Who determines the difference? 4. Would a beautiful person in this school be a beautiful person on the other side of the world? Vice versa? Explain your response in small groups. Read *Ugly* (de Maupassant, 1909). For each paragraph in *Ugly*, have students note their emotions with respect to the main character. **Postreading Discussion** 1. Who determines the ultimate standard for beauty in this short story? 2. How did your feelings about the main character evolve during this story? 3. How did your beliefs about beauty evolve during this story? 4. What specific words or phrases affected your understanding of beauty or ugliness as you read? 5. How are beauty or ugliness described and how are they considered beyond physical descriptions in this story? When? In what terms? *continued*

RL Standard 3 Grade 8, *continued*

Grade and Standard	Typical Learners	Advanced Learners
	Postreading Discussion	**Part II: Research**
	1. Identify characters in *Bad Boy* who functioned as teachers, literally and figuratively, with relation to the main character.	1. Ask students to select one of the following cultures and research the way beauty is defined:
	2. For each of the individuals identified as teachers, describe the qualities these individuals possessed that portrayed them as teachers.	• Asian, • South African, or • Middle Eastern
	3. How instructive were these individuals for the main character? What were the main "lessons" these characters had in the life of the main character?	2. Students will develop a presentation of their findings to share with a small group.
	4. Whose "lessons" were the most instructive for the main character? Use evidence from the text to support your view.	**Part III: Writing** Have students compare and contrast their definition of culture with that of the culture they researched.
	5. Which of these characters was the most instructive, or taught you the most through this memoir? Explain your response.	
	6. How are your actions instructive for others?	
	7. What are the life lessons you are passing on, and to whom are you teaching them?	

RL Standard 3 Grades 9–10

Connections to Writing and Speaking/Listening

CCSS.ELA-Literacy.Speaking/Listening.9–10.4: Present information, findings, and supporting evidence clearly, concisely, and logically such that listeners can follow the line of reasoning. The organization, development, substance, and style are appropriate to purpose, audience, and task.

CCSS.ELA-Literacy.Speaking/Listening.11–12.4: Present information, findings, and supporting evidence, conveying a clear and distinct perspective such that listeners can follow the line of reasoning. Alternative or opposing perspectives are addressed, and the organization, development, substance, and style are appropriate to purpose, audience, and a range of formal and informal tasks.

CCSS.ELA-Literacy.Writing.9–10.1: Write arguments to support claims in an analysis of substantive topics or texts, using valid reasoning and relevant and sufficient evidence.

CCSS.ELA-Literacy.Writing.11–12.1: Write arguments to support claims in an analysis of substantive topics or texts, using valid reasoning and relevant and sufficient evidence.

Implementation Considerations

Each of these steps will occur after students have finished reading *Macbeth*. The teacher will engage students in a large-group discussion. Students will work independently to draft the essay, and the teacher will provide individual guidance as needed in class for students as they develop this work.

The teacher will facilitate a debate. Depending on the class size, smaller groups may be formed for debates to allow time for more student interaction and verbal expression.

Differentiation Considerations

This learning experience was differentiated using:

- consideration of a complex concept and its role in the characters within a challenging text;
- development of a well-supported persuasive argument in an essay;
- product development and presentation for an authentic audience;
- infusion of multiple language arts standards;
- out-of-level objective (above level); and
- evaluation of character and defense of position using evidence from text to support.

Assessment Considerations

Text-based discussion may be assessed using the Middle and High School Critical Thinking Rubric (Great Books Foundation, n.d.b). The persuasive writing assignment may be scored using the Persuasive Writing Scoring Guide (ReadWriteThink, 2004). Debate may be assessed using the Classroom Debate Rubric (Winona State University, n.d.).

RL Standard 3 Grades 9–10

Grade and Standard	Typical Learners	Advanced Learners

Grades 9–10
Standard RL.9–10.3: Analyze how complex characters (e.g., those with multiple or conflicting motivations) develop over the course of a text, interact with other characters, and advance the plot or develop the theme.
	Part I
	Read *The Scarlett Letter* (Hawthorne, 1850/1994).
	
	Discussion
	1. Have students describe the following characters and their initial and final impressions of these characters:
	  • Hester Prynne
	  • Roger Chillingworth
	  • Aurthur Dimmesdale
	
	2. Have students describe the central plot developments that informed their characterization of these individuals.
	
	Part II: Writing
	  The American poet, Maya Angelou, has said "You may encounter many defeats, but you must not be defeated. In fact, it may be necessary to encounter the defeats, so you can know who you are, what you can rise from, how you can still come out of it" (see http://www.thinkexist.com/quotation/you_may_encounter_many_defeats-but_you_must_not/338144.html).
	  Based on Angelou's statement, students will write an essay defending how one of the central characters in *The Scarlet Letter* most exemplifies this credo. Ask students to use passages and references to the text to support their argument.
		Part I
		Read *Macbeth* (Shakespeare, 1606/2004).
		
		Discussion
		1. Describe Macbeth's relationship with Lady Macbeth at the beginning, middle, and end of the play.
		2. How do Macbeth's struggles with ambition affect his relationship with Lady Macbeth?
		3. Who is more ambitious—Lady Macbeth or Macbeth? Provide evidence from the text to support your claim.
		
		Part II: Writing
		  Ultimately, whose ambition was more destructive, Macbeth's or Lady Macbeth's? Have students write a persuasive essay that supports their position.
		
		Part III: Verbal Expression
		  Based on their reasoning in the essay above, have students debate which character is more destructive—Macbeth or Lady Macbeth.

RL Standard 4 Grade 3

Connections to Writing and Speaking/Listening

CCSS.ELA-Literacy.Speaking/Listening.3.1: Engage effectively in a range of collaborative discussions (one-on-one, in groups, and teacher-led) with diverse partners on grade 3 topics and texts, building on others' ideas and expressing their own clearly.

CCSS.ELA-Literacy.Writing.5.10: Write routinely over extended time frames (time for research, reflection, and revision) and shorter time frames (a single sitting or a day or two) for a range of discipline-specific tasks, purposes, and audiences.

Implementation Considerations

Following independent reading of the text, the teacher will facilitate a discussion of the questions in Part I with the whole group.

The teacher will then introduce the question in Part II and ask students to develop a response with textual support and share with a classmate. Following peer sharing, the teacher will invite students to share responses aloud with the class.

The teacher will provide the writing prompt and independent writing time for students to develop their poems. Then, the teacher will share student work samples to illustrate the various ways metaphor was included in student poems.

Differentiation Considerations

This learning experience was differentiated using:
- complex questions requiring careful textual analysis;
- consideration of a specific figurative language device;
- evaluation of a poem and justification for response;
- creation of an original product;
- presentation to an authentic audience;
- infusion of multiple language arts standards;

- accelerated standards for writing and speaking and listening; and
- out-of-level objective (above grade level).

Assessment Considerations

The assessment of these tasks may include a product assessment for the poem created and an observation tool for the think-aloud discussion questions.

RL Standard 4 Grade 3

Grade and Standard	Typical Learners	Advanced Learners
Grade 3 Standard RL.3.4: Determine the meaning of words and phrases as they are used in a text, distinguishing literal from nonliteral language.	**Part I** Read *The Moon's the North Wind's Cooky* (Lindsey, 1919). **Question for Discussion** 1. How does the author describe the South Wind and North Wind in the poem? 2. Complete a Venn diagram comparing the two winds. **Part II** Ask students to make a list of characteristics of an object. How could this object express human characteristics? For example: • A table has four legs. • A table has a flat surface. • A table can be used to gather people together. • Our kitchen table, with its weary legs and welcoming scars, brought us together and kept us connected each night. Have them create a description of an object that has human characteristics.	**Part I** Read *The Moon's the North Wind's Cooky* (Lindsey, 1919). **Questions for Discussion** 1. How is the South Wind different from the North Wind in this poem? What words specifically illustrate these differences? How does the author create a relationship between the North Wind and the South Wind? 2. Can the wind bite? Can it knead? Why does the author say the winds can bite or knead? 3. How do the words "bite" and "knead" sound different? How are the actions different? 4. If I ate cookies and left you only scraps, how would you feel about me? 5. If the person sitting next to you baked cookies for you each day, how would you feel about him or her? **Part II** Ask students what they think is the most powerful metaphor in this poem, and why. Have them share their thinking and support from the poem aloud with the class. **Part III: Presentation** Students will write a poem describing the personality of different crayons who live together in a box and incorporate metaphor in this poem. The teacher will project the poems of three students for classmates to identify the use of metaphor.

RL Standard 4 Grade 5

Connections to Writing and Speaking/Listening

CCSS.ELA-Literacy.Speaking/Listening.5.1: Engage effectively in a range of collaborative discussions (one-on-one, in groups, and teacher-led) with diverse partners on grade 5 topics and texts, building on others' ideas and expressing their own clearly.

CCSS.ELA-Literacy.Speaking/Listening.7.6: Adapt speech to a variety of contexts and tasks, demonstrating command of formal English when indicated or appropriate.

CCSS.ELA-Literacy.Writing.7.9: Draw evidence from literary or informational texts to support analysis, reflection, and research.

Implementation Considerations

To introduce the topic of the moon, the teacher should project several images of the moon (various sizes, shapes, illustrations). Then students will independently write descriptions of the moon to be shared with partners following a 5-minute think time.

The teacher will read the poem "Moon" while students follow along in text. Then, the teacher will facilitate discussion of the questions provided in Part I, asking students to support responses with textual references when appropriate.

Students will develop individual lists of several objects, then generate a list of descriptors for one of these objects.

Using these descriptors, students will develop poems that incorporate figurative language, such as similes, metaphors, or personification. The teacher will monitor individual writing progress, offering support and feedback to each student as he or she develops his or her poem. Students will practice reciting their poems in preparation for the poetry sharing.

While students recite poems, the teacher may simultaneously project the students' work. Classmates should give examples of figurative language from peer poems.

Differentiation Considerations

This learning experience was differentiated using:
- development and presentation of a product;
- infusion of multiple language arts standards;
- accelerated standards for writing and speaking and listening;
- out–of–level objective (above grade level); and
- choices provided in writing.

Assessment Considerations

Poetry reading will be assessed according to the *Poetry Out Loud Scoring Rubric* (Poetry Out Loud, 2012). Text analysis of poetry may be assessed. Teachers may also evaluate the student's identification of figurative language in poetry.

RL Standard 4 Grade 5

Grade and Standard	Typical Learners	Advanced Learners
Grade 5 Standard RL.5.4 Determine the meaning of words and phrases as they are used in a text, including figurative language such as metaphors and similes.	**Part I** Read "The New Colossus" (Lazarus, 1883). On a chart with three columns, have students put the original figurative word or phrase. In the second column, put the literal version. In the third column, have students make a qualitative reader-response comment on the ways in which the poem alludes to historical and current places and issues. Engage the students in a collaborative discussion about the ways in which figurative language enhanced their experience and understanding of the poem. **Part II** 1. What is the narrator's attitude toward the Statue of Liberty? 2. Students should identify specific lines and phrases from the poem to support their claims. 3. Provide students with background information about the Statue of Liberty: Streaming video of "The Statue of Liberty" (History Channel, 2013a); video of "Statue of Liberty" (History Channel, 2013b); and Statue of Liberty facts and e-tour (National Park Service, 2013). **Part III: Writing** 1. How does knowing the historical context of this poem affect your understanding of it? 2. Reread the poem and, for each line, write how you are thinking about the line now that you know the context versus how you initially interpreted the meaning before knowing this context. 3. In pairs, share your responses to each line from your notes.	**Part I** Prereading: Write a description of the moon. Read "Moon" (Stevenson, 1885/1913). **Discussion Questions** 1. What does it mean for the moon to have a face like the clock in the hall? 2. Do trees have forks? Do birds sleep in forks? 3. Is the moon a woman? Why would the author call the moon "she"? 4. What is a harbor quay? How is it different from the other places described in this poem? 5. Why does the author describe so many different places? **Part II: Writing** 1. Identify a list of some of your favorite objects, whether these are items that belong to you or are found in nature. 2. Choose one of these objects and create a list of words and phrases that come to mind when you think of this object. 3. Using this list of words and phrases, create a poem that incorporates similes, metaphors, and/or personification. **Part III: Verbal Expression** In a classwide poetry reading, students will present their poems. Classmates will identify the use of figurative language included in each student's poem.

RL Standard 4 Grade 8

Connections to Writing and Speaking/Listening

CCSS.ELA-Literacy.Speaking/Listening.8.1: Engage effectively in a range of collaborative discussions (one-on-one, in groups, and teacher-led) with diverse partners on grade 8 topics, texts, and issues, building on others' ideas and expressing their own clearly.

CCSS.ELA-Literacy.Writing.8.1: Write arguments to support claims with clear reasons and relevant evidence.

Implementation Considerations

The teacher will post and read the prereading prompt and allow individual writing time. In small groups, students will discuss their independent writing responses. Following small-group discussions, the teacher will facilitate large-group discussion of the discussion questions provided.

The teacher will post and pose the prompt in Part II. Students will work independently to develop a poem, then create an illustration representative of their poem. Each of these experiences may be completed for homework or in class as preparation for sharing with the large group.

Students will provide their illustrations while reciting their poem. Following the recitation, students will explain how their illustration captures the nuances of their poem.

Differentiation Considerations

This learning experience was differentiated using:
- creative production in development of a poem that includes personification;
- product presentation through poetry reading;
- infusion of multiple language arts standards; and
- accelerated standards for writing and speaking and listening.

Assessment Considerations

The poetry presentation assignment will be assessed using an oral presentation rubric (ReadWriteThink, 2010). The essay may be evaluated using an expository essay rubric.

RL Standard 4 Grade 8

Grade and Standard	Typical Learners	Advanced Learners
Grade 8 Standard RL.8.4: Determine the meaning of words and phrases as they are used in a text, including figurative and connotative meanings; analyze the impact of specific word choices on meaning and tone, including analogies or allusions to other texts.	**Part I** Think of a historical figure who made a controversial decision. As a class, generate a list of examples of historical figures and their controversial decisions/actions. Read "The Road Not Taken" (Frost, 1916/2009). **Postreading Discussion Questions** 1. What images came to mind as you read this poem? 2. What words from the poem activated these images in your mind's eye? 3. What meanings does Frost convey with the word "road"? 4. What are the "roads" the historical figures we listed above took? 5. What is the speaker's attitude toward his or her selection of roads? Identify specific lines from the text to support this tone. **Part II: Writing** Ask students: What is the personal message you take from "The Road Not Taken"? **Part III: Verbal Expression** In small groups, discuss: 1. The personal meaning you found in "The Road Not Taken." 2. Who should read this poem and why you feel they should read it.	**Part I: Prewriting** Students will identify two inanimate objects (e.g., a tree, a ball, a mirror, a backpack, or a watch) and describe how these objects are similar. Then think about how one of these objects is like freedom, like happiness, or like loneliness. On their own, write a few descriptions that convey how the inanimate object they've identified might reflect one of those concepts. Students will post the inanimate object and their list of words and phrases for personification for classmates to read. They will offer additional ideas to classmates' inanimate object personification phrases. Read "I Am the Moon" (Fletcher, 2012). **Postreading Discussion Questions** 1. Who is "I" in line 2? How do you know this? 2. What is the author's attitude toward the moon? What word or phrase conveys this to you the most? 3. How does the author use figurative language to describe the sun? **Part II: Writing** 1. Students will write a poem that incorporates personification of the school building or other inanimate object. 2. Students will create an illustration to accompany their poem that demonstrates the personification of the object. **Part III: Verbal Expression** 1. Students will present their poem and illustration of their poem to the class. 2. Following the recitation of their original poem, have students explain how their illustration reflects an aspect of their poem.

RL Standard 4 Grades 9–10

Connections to Writing and Speaking/Listening

CCSS.ELA-Literacy.Writing.9–10.2: Write informative/explanatory texts to examine and convey complex ideas, concepts, and information clearly and accurately through the effective selection, organization, and analysis of content.

CCSS.ELA-Literacy.Speaking/Listening.11–12.1: Initiate and participate effectively in a range of collaborative discussions (one-on-one, in groups, and teacher-led) with diverse partners on grades 11–12 topics, texts, and issues, building on others' ideas, and expressing their own clearly and persuasively.

CCSS.ELA-Literacy.Writing.11–12.2: Write informative/explanatory texts to examine and convey complex ideas, concepts, and information clearly and accurately through the effective selection, organization, and analysis of content.

Implementation Considerations

Students will independently read "If." The teacher will facilitate large-group discussion of questions posed in Part I. The teacher will distribute and read the prompt, and students will write essays. The teacher will convene students in small groups to discuss the main ideas from their "ifs" essays and discuss with classmates. Following the small-group discussions, the teacher will convene the class to share the various "ifs" discussed. Then, the teacher will facilitate a large-group discussion of literary characters or modern-day figures who exemplify "ifs" discussed in small groups. Students should explain how the figure or character exemplifies the "if."

Differentiation Considerations

This learning experience was differentiated using:
- evaluation of a poem according to personal beliefs;
- justification of evaluations in conversations with peers;

- relating concepts from literary work to the current-day world with sound explanations to support assertions;
- infusion of multiple language arts standards;
- accelerated standards for writing and speaking and listening; and
- out-of-level objective (above grade level).

Assessment Considerations

Essays may be evaluated using expository writing rubrics. Students may self-assess small-group contributions in speaking, listening, and considering multiple perspectives, and the teacher may evaluate student contributions in the large-group discussion according to textual support for claims offered, verbal expression of ideas, response to different views, and connections to the ideas of classmates.

RL Standard 4 Grades 9–10

Grade and Standard	Typical Learners	Advanced Learners

Grade 9–10
 	
RL.9–10.4: Determine the meaning of words and phrases as they are used in the text, including figurative and connotative meanings; analyze the cumulative impact of specific word choices on meaning and tone (e.g., how the language evokes a sense of time and place; how it sets a formal or informal tone).
	Part I
	Read *Julius Caesar* (Shakespeare, 2003). Students should follow along in the text and use any available text aids to facilitate comprehension. Stop periodically to check for comprehension:
	
	1. How is Julius Caesar viewed at this stage of the play?
	2. Describe Julius Caesar based on his actions and statements in Act I.
	3. What evidence do you have from the text to support these characterizations?
	4. What is the "mood" of this first act, and what sort of tone does this set for the next act?
	
	Part II: Writing
	Ask students to paraphrase:
	
	1. "Oh you hard hearts, you cruel men of Rome/ Knew you not Pompey?"
	2. "These growing feathers plucked from Caesar's wings/ Will make him fly an ordinary pitch."
	
	In an essay, students should identify the three most important life lessons for teens that can be drawn from *Julius Caesar*.
		Part I
		Read: "If" (Kipling, 1910/2013).
		
		Discussion Questions
		1. What is the meaning of:
		  • "If you can keep your head when all about you/ Are losing theirs and blaming it on you"?
		  • "If you can meet triumph and disaster/ And treat those two imposters just the same"?
		  • "If you can talk with crowds and keep your virtue, or walk with kings—nor lose the common touch"?
		
		2. What sort of emotion does the author wish to convey in this poem? What evidence from the poem creates this effect?
		
		Part II: Writing
		Ask students to identify three "ifs" within this poem that speak the most to their life values and to describe these values in an essay.
		
		Part III: Verbal Expression
		In small groups, have students discuss one of the "ifs" that resonated so much with them and their value system.
		Students will identify a literary character or current-day individual who exemplifies one of their ifs and explain how this individual has done so.

RL Standard 9 Grade 3

Connections to Writing and Speaking/Listening

CCSS.ELA-Literacy.Writing.4.9: Draw evidence from literary or informational texts to support analysis, reflection, and research.

CCSS.ELA-Literacy.Speaking/Listening.3.3: Ask and answer questions about information from a speaker, offering appropriate elaboration and detail.

Implementation Considerations

These activities will take at least three periods to complete. Students will create their narrative outside of class. The teacher will group students by reading ability to do Part I. Individual responses will be elicited for Parts II and III. Monitoring of student journal writing should be done to ensure focus on task; group work should be monitored for engagement of all learners in each group.

Differentiation Considerations

This learning experience was differentiated using:
- choice of author and text,
- greater complexity in questions and activities, and
- use of creative products.

Assessment Considerations

The assessment of this task demand may include a narrative writing rubric and a presentation rubric.

RL Standard 9 Grade 3

Grade and Standard	Typical Learners	Advanced Learners
Grade 3 RL.3.9 Compare and contrast the themes, settings, and plots of stories written by the same author about the same or similar characters (e.g., in books from a series).	Select an author to study based on third-grade text. For example, select books in a series written by the same author, such as The Boxcar Children Mysteries by Gertrude Warner (2010). Students will select two books in the series to compare and contrast. Students will read the books and create a Venn diagram or T-chart to make their comparisons. Students will write a narrative using their Venn diagram. Writings may be published and shared with others.	**Part I** 1. Ask students to read aloud in class in small groups three books by Verna Aardema, an author who explores the Masai tribe in Africa and their struggles to survive as well as their customs and beliefs. 2. After reading the three tales, ask students in small groups to complete a comparison chart on the plot, setting, and themes of each story. 3. Students may report from each group on their findings. **Part II: Writing** 　Use the work charts produced to have students explore the theme of tribal behavior in the Masai in a journal reflection. Think about why it is important. How and why does the behavior get passed on from one generation to the next? What are some consequences of the behavior that are positive; what might be negative ones? (This may call for a 20-minute in-class writing assignment.) Now ask students to research important ideas about the Masai tribe and add these ideas to their reflection response. **Part III: Speaking/Listening** 　The choice of words in the Aardema stories and the rhythms associated with the language employed make the sound of the stories very interesting. Students will create a story that uses rhythmic language to make its point. Ask students to create a character, plot, and setting as a backdrop to the language they employ. Share students' stories in class.

RL Standard 9 Grade 5

Connections to Writing and Speaking/Listening

CCSS.ELA-Literacy.Writing.5.1: Write narratives to develop real or imagined experiences or events using effective technique, descriptive details, and clear event sequences.

CCSS.ELA-Literacy.Speaking/Listening.5.3: Use knowledge of language and its conventions when writing, speaking, reading, or listening.

Implementation Considerations

This activity set will take at least three periods to complete. Each segment should be completed during class time. Group work should be monitored by the teacher through questioning during the construction of the visual.

Differentiation Considerations

This learning experience was differentiated using:
- author and reading choices,
- complexity of language demands, and
- more abstraction in respect to author style.

Assessment Considerations

The use of a standard form for persuasive writing should be employed, with additional criteria added for a peer assessment that addresses the criteria of word choice and quality of syntax.

RL Standard 9 Grade 5

Grade and Standard	Typical Learners	Advanced Learners

Grade 5
RL.5.9: Compare and contrast stories in the same genre (e.g., mysteries and adventure stories) on their approaches to similar themes and topics.
	Choose a relevant topic or event about which your students could write a narrative (field day, a school celebration, a field trip). Alternatively, you could stage an event (for example, have someone come into the room, do three jumping jacks, blow a whistle, recite a poem, and leave). After the event, ask students to write a descriptive narrative about what they saw or experienced. Have several students share their accounts aloud, noting main points on chart paper. Engage students in a discussion about the differences in style (and even the differences in the facts) of each narrative. How do they think the personality of each writer influenced their perception of events? Did their seat in the class or vantage point influence their perception? What other factors can we consider in how a writer crafts his approach to a theme or topic?	**Part I**
		   Edgar Allen Poe was a master storyteller in the genre of horror and its depiction in stories. Ask students to select and read two Poe (2013) stories from the following list:
		• *The Tell-Tale Heart,*
		• *The Cask of Amontillado,*
		• *The Masque of the Red Death,* or
		• *The Pit and the Pendulum.*
		
		Then ask them to answer the following questions in assigned groups:
		1. What are the similarities of these two stories in respect to theme, plot, character delineation, and setting? Display your results in a visual.
		2. What can you say about Poe's style of writing, based on both stories read?
		
		Have groups report out and share their visuals. Discuss the second question as a whole group.
		
		Part II: Writing
		   Have students write an argument for their friends to convince them to read Poe. What literary devices can they employ to build interest in their argument? What word choice will heighten interest? What grammatical structures (use of varied sentence patterns, use of phrases and clauses, etc.) will heighten attention to their writing?
		
		Part III: Speaking/Listening
		   Have students share their persuasive essays on Poe with the class. Ask students to assess the strength of the arguments mounted, word choice, and the quality of the syntax for each paper presented.

RL Standard 9 Grade 8

Connections to Writing and Speaking/Listening

CCSS.ELA-Literacy.Writing.8.3: Write narratives to develop real or imagined experiences or events using effective technique, relevant descriptive details, and well-structured event sequences.

CCSS.ELA-Literacy.Speaking/Listening.8.1: Engage effectively in a range of collaborative discussions (one-on-one, in groups, and teacher-led) with diverse partners on grade 8 topics, texts, and issues, building on others' ideas and expressing their own clearly.

Implementation Considerations

This task demand may be implemented using small groups for the discussion within a class period. A second period will be needed to engage dyads in the project work. Teachers may want to ensure that students are successfully analyzing the three art forms via the class discussion by using question probes as follow-up for some questions.

Differentiation Considerations

This learning experience was differentiated using:
- out-of-level objectives;
- more advanced poetry;
- high level of complexity, including comparative analyses of three art forms; and
- high demand for creativity.

Assessment Considerations

Student products should be judged according to the following criteria:
- interpretation of the myth selected in both words and images;

- quality of the products;
- use of creative and innovative ideas;
- use of effective images in both the poem and the illustration;
- effective discussion of artistic elements employed; and
- command of language mechanics (i.e., spelling, grammar and usage).

RL Standard 9 Grade 8

Grade and Standard	Typical Learners	Advanced Learners
Grade 8 RL.8.9 Analyze how a modern work of fiction draws on themes, patterns of events, or character types from myths, traditional stories, or religious works such as the Bible, including describing how the material is rendered new.	**Part I** Have students read the myth of Daedalus and Icarus from an online source (http://www.island-ikaria.com/culture/myth.asp). Discuss the myth, using the following questions: 1. What pattern does the myth follow? 2. What aspects of human behavior does the myth demonstrate? 3. Icarus tries out the wings that his father Daedalus created that eventually are responsible for his demise. What aspects of being creative or innovative are being explored here? What lessons are learned? 4. What lessons are revealed about fathers and sons? **Part II** Now ask students to read the William Carlos Williams (1985) poem called "Landscape With the Fall of Icarus." Discuss the following questions, based on the poem: *continued*	**Part I** Have students read the myth of Daedalus and Icarus from the website listed in the Typical Learners section. Discuss the myth, using the following questions: 1. What purpose did this myth serve for ancient Greeks and Romans? 2. What was its moral? 3. What pattern does the myth follow? 4. What aspects of human behavior does the myth demonstrate? 5. Icarus tries out the wings that his father Daedalus created that eventually are responsible for his demise. What aspects of being creative or innovative are being explored here? What lessons are learned? 6. What lessons are revealed about fathers and sons? 7. How does the style of the writing contribute to the telling of the myth? **Part II** Now ask students to read the William Carlos Williams (1985) poem "Landscape With the Fall of Icarus." Discuss the following questions, based on the poem: 1. What words are important in conveying the tone of the poem? 2. What images that Williams uses are the most powerful? Why? 3. What is the theme of this poem? 4. How do you react to it? *continued*

RL Standard 9 Grade 8, *continued*

Grade and Standard	Typical Learners	Advanced Learners
	Regarding the poem: 1. What words are important in conveying the tone of the poem? 2. What images that Williams uses are the most powerful? Why? 3. What is the theme of this poem? 4. How do you react to it? **Part III** Now project the image of the Pieter Bruegel painting "Landscape with the Fall of Icarus" on the projector or LCD screen and ask students to study it as a visual depiction of the event. Ask students to write a journal entry, comparing the depiction of Icarus in the painting and poem. What is similar and what is different in each artist's representation?	5. What structural devices does Williams use to heighten the impact of his poem? **Part III: Speaking/Listening** Now project the image of the Pieter Bruegel painting "Landscape With the Fall of Icarus" on the projector or LCD screen and ask students to study it as a visual depiction of the event. Regarding the comparison of myth, picture, and poem, ask students: 1. How do Williams and Bruegel each interpret the myth? Are there distinctions in their interpretation that reflect the different time periods in which they worked? 2. How does each artist extend the myth for the audience of their time? 3. Both the writer and the painter were working in innovative forms in their art when they did these works. What aspects of creativity do you see in each product? 4. Read about Bruegel and Williams with respect to their work. Analyze the similarities and differences in artist and author style. (Adapted from The Indiana High Ability Project [HAP], 2013.) **Part IV: Writing** Have students select a Roman myth of their choice and create a poem and illustration that depicts that myth, using a modern form of poetry. Have them write an artist's statement about key aspects of interpretation (i.e., theme, vocabulary, structure, images and symbols).

RL Standard 9 Grades 9–10

Connections to Writing and Speaking/Listening

CCSS.ELA-Literacy.Writing.9–10.1: Write arguments to support claims in an analysis of substantive topics or texts, using valid reasoning and relevant and sufficient evidence.

CCSS.ELA-Literacy.Speaking/Listening.9–10.5: Make strategic use of digital media (e.g., textual, graphical, audio, visual, and interactive elements) in presentations to enhance understanding of and add interest to findings, reasoning, and evidence.

Implementation Considerations

Students will need at least four periods to complete this activity set. Work on their self-selected mythic hero will need to be done outside of class.

Differentiation Considerations

This learning experience was differentiated using:
- greater complexity in the writing task,
- more creative response in the mythic hero narrative; and
- greater challenge for writing.

Assessment Considerations

The in-class writing assignment will be assessed using the persuasive writing model rubric. The hero cycle project will be assessed using a rubric that examines the dimensions of the accuracy of the mythic stages, the aptness of the connections made to the cycle, and the generalizable characteristics of the hero selected to other individuals.

RL Standard 9 Grades 9–10

Grade and Standard	Typical Learners	Advanced Learners
Grade 9–10 RL.9–10.9: Analyze how an author draws on and transforms source material in a specific work (e.g., how Shakespeare treats a theme or topic from Ovid or the Bible or how a later author draws on a play by Shakespeare).	**Part I** Read the play *Julius Caesar* by William Shakespeare (2003). **Part II** Distribute a timeline on Julius Caesar's life. • Discuss the differences between the facts of Caesar's life and the legends/myths about his life. • Analyze Shakespeare's language in the play by examining selected soliloquies. • Discuss the major themes in the play. • Return to the discussion of *tragic heroes* and *tragic flaws*. Ask the students for current real-world examples of tragic heroes and their flaws. • Each reading group will take 5 minutes to share their presentations to the class.	**Part I** Read the sections of *The Iliad* by Homer (1260 BC/1998) about the death of Achilles. Discuss the following questions in a Socratic seminar: 1. What are the features of a tragic hero that Achilles represents? 2. How are these qualities also used by Shakespeare in *Macbeth*? 3. Modern literature features the antihero rather than a tragic hero. How are they different? What might be some examples? **Part II: Writing** Students will construct a 40-minute persuasive essay on the following prompt: *There are no universal qualities of a hero that transcend time and culture.* **Part III: Speaking/Listening** Using multimedia, ask students to present their archetypal hero, chosen from literature of any period or from modern life. What are the key qualities, deeds, challenges and obstacles overcome, and insights gained by this hero? Students will create a mythic cycle to justify their argument (i.e., the hero, the journey, the challenge, the response, the final insight/understanding).

Reading Informational Text Examples

Transition From Reading Literature Examples

As we move from the examples in the literature section of the standards to the informational text examples, it may be helpful for the reader to note some important distinctions between the two sets of examples. First of all, websites are frequently provided for reading material in the information text section while they have not been in the literature section. The use of resources in the informational text section requires resource citations in order to make it viable while the literature section is rooted in the use of classic and contemporary literature that is more accessible in various forms. Secondly, the examples in the informational text section are often provided in the content areas of social studies and science, demonstrating the cross-disciplinary nature of these standards for reading across the curriculum. In contrast, the literature standards' examples are all genre-based literature in short story, poetry, or essay form. Finally, the informational text examples often focus on multiple resources that require students to cross over types of readings and viewings in order to meet the standard.

Overview of the Reading for Informational Examples

The following examples, which represent appropriate-level activities for typical and advanced students, focus on several aspects of differentiation. The activities for advanced learners are more abstract and idea-based than what would be expected for typical learners. They are more complex, requiring gifted learners to think at multiple levels simultaneously and work with more variables than the typical learner. By providing product choice, they also provide a creative context for advanced learners to express innovative ideas.

The activities for gifted learners are designed to be conducted in a self-contained, pull-out, or inclusive setting with a small group of gifted students in which the activities have been "tiered" with this activity as part of a differentiated classroom. Lessons may take place over several months or in single class periods. The important factor is that gifted and advanced students have opportunities to work together and engage in meaningful work.

In addition to connecting to the CCSS-ELA Writing and Speaking/Listening standards, the example learning experiences are interdisciplinary, created in the following ways:

- Standard RI.2 was integrated with the study of biography—particularly one of a scientist;
- Standard RI.3 was integrated with social studies;
- Standard RI.4 was integrated with the Next Generation Science Standards; and
- Standard RI.9 was integrated with social studies.

Sample Differentiated Learning Experiences in Reading Informational Text Standards

RI Standard 2 Grade 3

Connections to Writing and Speaking/Listening

CCSS.ELA-Literacy.Writing.3.2: Write informative/explanatory texts to examine a topic to convey ideas and information clearly.

CCSS.ELA-Literacy.Writing.3.7: Conduct short research projects that build knowledge about a topic.

CCSS.ELA-Literacy.Speaking/Listening.3.4: Report on a topic or text, tell a story, or recount an experience with appropriate facts and relevant, descriptive details, speaking clearly at an understandable pace.

Connections to Interdisciplinary Standards

Science 3-ESS2a: Organize simple weather data sets to record local weather data and identify day-to-day weather variations, as well as long-term patterns of weather.

Math 3.3: Draw a scaled picture graph and a scaled bar graph to represent a data set with several categories. Solve one-or two-step "how many more" and "how many less" problems using information presented in scaled bar graphs.

Implementation Considerations

Students will independently read *The Man Who Named the Clouds* in addition to *Cloud Dance*. The teacher will facilitate large-group discussion of questions posed in Part I. The teacher will distribute the graph paper and encourage different groups of students to collect different data over time. Advanced students should be responsible for collecting the advanced material. The advanced math of correlational data should also be presented. The teacher will convene students in small groups to discuss the interpretation of their data and discuss with classmates. Following the small-group discussions, the teacher will convene the class to share various data analyses and each group should contribute its data toward a whole-class presentation of weather. If the class is inclusive, lower groups will cover more basic information while the advanced groups will cover the more complex material. If the class is a group of advanced students, connections between advanced material and more basic weather concepts should be delineated.

Differentiation Considerations

This learning experience was differentiated using:
- advanced math content, using correlations to determine relationships and implications;
- complexity of information by including the biographical aspect;
- critical and creative thinking through an examination of the concept of patterns; and
- integration and use of science concepts/understandings within literacy activities.

Assessment Considerations

Presentations should be assessed through an adapted rubric that includes elements of:

- extensive use of content, to include use and explanation of correlational data;
- analysis of the inductive/deductive process used by Mr. Howard; and
- analysis of the relationship between barometric pressure, types of clouds observed, and precipitation.

Care should be taken that the assessment reflects the medium of the product as well as the content-related embodiment of the program goals. Students should self-assess that the presentation follows acceptable presentation guidelines of readability, size, use of visuals, etc.

RI Standard 2 Grade 3

Grade and Standard	Typical Learners	Advanced Learners
Grade 3 RI.3.2: Determine the main idea of a text and recount key details that support that idea.	Read *Cloud Dance* by Thomas Locker (2003). Have students graph weather charts, taking temperature, humidity, barometric pressure and precipitation measures on a daily basis. Students will visually present findings on local typical weather and explain how the weather changes over time at their location. Students will provide main ideas of the text and supporting details of the types of clouds, using the information from *Cloud Dance* through a PowerPoint or Prezi.	Read *Cloud Dance* and *The Man who Named the Clouds* by Julie Hanna and Joan Holub (2006). Have students graph weather charts as well, drawing implications for barometric pressure and noting correlations between barometric pressures and ensuing types of cloud cover. Questions to be asked might include: 1. What are the implications of weather changes? 2. Who needs to know about weather changes and why? 3. What patterns in temperature, cloud cover, and barometric pressure do you observe? Provide examples. Using the main ideas and supporting details in the text about Luke Howard, students will describe what information Mr. Howard used and the process he used to describe and name the different types of clouds, relating his types of clouds presented to the weather data they have gathered, using a PowerPoint or Prezi. Impact of his work on current-day meteorologists should be explored.

RI Standard 2 Grade 5

Connections to Writing and Speaking/Listening

CCSS.ELA-Literacy.Writing.5.2: Write informative/explanatory texts to examine a topic and convey ideas and information clearly.

CCSS.ELA-Literacy.Writing.5.7: Conduct short research projects that use several sources to build knowledge through investigation of different aspects of a topic.

CCSS.ELA-Literacy.Speaking/Listening.5.4: Report on a topic or text or present an opinion, sequencing ideas logically and using appropriate facts and relevant, descriptive details to support main ideas or themes; speak clearly at an understandable pace.

Connection to Interdisciplinary Standards

Science 5PS4-a: Apply scientific knowledge of how lenses bend light to design a tool to enhance vision.

Implementation Considerations

In an inclusive setting, the advanced students should be pulled into a smaller group to research how the telescope was used to discover the Big Bang Theory. Students can explore beyond how telescopes work to how the data that they demonstrate can be interpreted. All students should contribute to a presentation that explores the use of telescopes. In an advanced class, the parts of the telescope should be reviewed, but the majority of instruction should focus on the use and interpretation of data from telescopes. It is expected that advanced students will explore the speed of light and how telescopes are used to see into the past. The words from The Big Bang Theory theme song can be used to supplement this instruction through multimedia.

Differentiation Considerations

This activity was differentiated using grade-level concepts of telescopes and space, but also included:

- advanced content of science to incorporate information on galaxies and the Big Bang Theory;
- more complex content through the inclusion of the biographical aspect; and
- a focus on critical and creative thinking by an examination of the concept of time and its relationship to light.

Assessment Considerations

The presentation should be evaluated using a rubric for the appropriate format. A typical student's rubric should be supplemented with elements that include advanced content applications, specifically:

- understanding of the Big Bang Theory's connection to telescopes, and
- descriptions of the behavior of light.

In addition, advanced students should be expected to present their material in a way that demonstrates the complexity of the content. A greater degree of connections should be provided through an adapted rubric.

RI Standard 2 Grade 5

Grade and Standard	Typical Learners	Advanced Learners
Grade 5 RI.5.2: Determine two or more main ideas of a text and explain how they are supported by key details; summarize the text.	Read: • *Close Encounters: Exploring the Universe with the Hubble Space Telescope* by Elaine Scott (1998), and • *Making and Enjoying Telescopes* by Robert Miller and Kenneth Wilson (1997). Using main ideas and supporting details from the text, students will create a telescope using descriptions from the book *Making and Enjoying Telescopes*. Have students demonstrate the steps necessary and explain how the telescope works, through a presentation format. Include details using the Hubble telescope for data and information.	Read: • *Edwin Hubble: Discoverer of Galaxies* by Claire Datnow (1997), and • *The Day We Found the Universe* by Marcia Bartusik (2010). Listen to and read: • *The Big Bang Theory* music and lyrics by Barenaked Ladies (2013). Using main ideas and supporting details from the text, students will describe how Hubble used his telescope to describe the universe and what information led him to understanding the nature of the galaxies and the Big Bang Theory. Advanced students will research the relationship between telescopes and the behavior of light as it relates to time. Have students present the use of the telescope in the discovery of the Big Bang theory using a Prezi or PowerPoint that includes links to the Internet and hyperlinks.

RI Standard 2 Grade 8

Connections to Writing and Speaking/Listening

CCSS.ELA-Literacy.Writing.8.2: Write informative/explanatory text to examine a topic and convey ideas, concepts, and information through the selection, organization, and analysis of relevant content.

CCSS.ELA-Literacy.Speaking/Listening.8.4: Present claims and findings, emphasizing salient points in a focused, coherent manner with relevant evidence, sound valid reasoning, and well-chosen details; use appropriate eye contact, adequate volume, and clear pronunciation.

Implementation Considerations

The first level of analysis of the text should focus on structure and comprehension. How does Douglass tell his story? What details does he include to provide depth to the story structure? How might this autobiographical account be similar and different from other autobiographical stories? How does the literary element of conflict appear in autobiography in ways that are similar to conflict's role in fiction?

The second level of analysis should focus on the concept of identity. Analysis of the abstract concept of identity may require some scaffolding activities. Teachers may lead group discussions on what an identity is and how a person might develop an identity. Additionally, students may write about events or relationships in their own lives that contributed to their identity development.

During conceptual analysis, the instructional goal is to extract the concept of identity out of Douglass's autobiography and discuss how each of us forms an identity. What is the role of conflict in identity development? What forces shaped Douglass's identity and how might this be generalized to how all people understand identity?

Differentiation Considerations

This learning experience was differentiated using:
- more complex products;
- complexity of analysis, which is created by adding conceptual understanding of identity and conflict to the analysis of the autobiography; and
- complexity to grade-level essay and speech expectations by requiring learners to state and defend their understanding of how conflict shapes identity in both the autobiography and reflection on their own lives.

Assessment Considerations

Students will create two products that could be assessed, the explanatory essay and the speech. Both of those products should be assessed according to standards of writing and speaking as well as conceptual understandings of autobiography, conflict, and identity.

RI Standard 2 Grade 8

Grade and Standard	Typical Learners	Advanced Learners
Grade 8 RI.8.2: Determine a central idea of a text and analyze its development over the course of the text, including the relationship to supporting ideas; provide an objective summary of the text.	Students will read Chapter 1 of *A Narrative of the Life of Frederick Douglass* (1845/1995) and summarize how Douglass describes the relationship between master and slave.	Students will read Chapter 1 of *A Narrative of the Life of Frederick Douglass* (1845/1995) and analyze the concept of identity through Douglass's description of his early life. An additional level of differentiation could be added by selecting an above-grade-level autobiography appropriate for gifted learners. For instance: *Autobiography: The Story of My Experiments With Truth* by Mohandas Ghandi (1927/2008), *Night* by Elie Wiesel (1955/2006), *The Autobiography of Malcolm X* by Malcolm X (1965/2001), or *The Autobiography of Benjamin Franklin* (1791/1996). Students will create an explanatory text in which they define the concept of identity and use textual evidence to explain how Douglass supports this concept of identity development in his autobiographical text. Students will prepare a speech on the topic of their own autobiography and the interaction of conflict and identity development.

RI Standard 2 Grades 9–10

Connection to Writing and Speaking/Listening

CCSS.ELA-Literacy.Writing.9-10.1: Write arguments to support claims in an analysis of substantive topics or texts, using valid reasoning and relevant and sufficient evidence.

CCSS.ELA-Literacy.Speaking/Listening.9-10.5: Make strategic use of digital media (e.g., textual, graphical, audio, visual, and interactive elements) in presentations to enhance understanding of and add interest to findings, reasoning, and evidence.

Implementation Considerations

Meditations on First Philosophy can be a complex text even for high-ability high school students. To provide scaffolding, the teacher may want to teach the students some background on the intellectual issues of the Enlightenment, including skepticism, empiricism, and rationalism. Alternatively, students could do some group or independent research on these topics as a way of building background knowledge.

There are six meditations in the book. The teacher may want to be more actively involved in helping students analyze Descartes' position in the first meditation and let the students grow in their independence of analysis through the remaining meditations.

Students should analyze one meditation at a time. Then, after the sixth meditation, they should determine the fundamental argument of the text as a whole. There may be more than one interpretation of the central idea of the meditations and students should be encouraged to explore multiple meanings.

Differentiation Considerations

This learning experience was differentiated using:

- greater text complexity, as well as the interdisciplinary connection to philosophical topics of epistemology and rationality; and
- an emphasis on advanced critical-thinking skills.

Assessment Considerations

The assessment focus should be on the students' ability to identify and provide evidence for the central idea the author develops throughout the text. Even though this is a complex text, the students should be able to determine and demonstrate the central idea.

To assess students' writing, utilize appropriate rubrics for writing argumentative essays using well-reasoned arguments and textual evidence to support claims. To assess students' audio-visual presentation, focus on standards of presentation to include design and speaking elements.

RI Standard 2 Grades 9–10

Grade and Standard	Typical Learners	Advanced Learners
Grades 9–10 RI.9–10.2. Determine a central idea of a text and analyze its development over the course of the text, including how it emerges and is shaped and refined by specific details, and provide a summary of the text.	Students will read a biographical text such as *Night* by Elie Wiesel (1955/2006), *The Autobiography of Malcolm X* (1965/2001), or *The Autobiography of Benjamin Franklin* (1791/1996) and describe how the author identifies a central idea to develop throughout the text.	Students will read *Meditations on First Philosophy* by Descartes (1641/1993). Students will identify a central idea that Descartes develops over the course of the text including detailed examples of how the author presents the central idea and how this central idea might help a young person think more clearly in the 21st century. Alternate texts that could be used for a similar learning task include Plato's (380 BC/2000) *The Republic* or Albert Camus's (1942/2005) *Myth of Sisyphus*. Students will write a persuasive essay in which they take a position that Descartes either "got it right" or "got it wrong" on his central idea. Students will develop the thesis with text evidence and well-reasoned argumentation. Students will create an audio-visual presentation in which they briefly summarize the text and present the central idea that Descartes develops.

RI Standard 3 Grade 3

Connections to Writing and Speaking/Listening

CCSS.ELA-Literacy.Writing.3.2: Write informative/explanatory texts to examine a topic to convey ideas and information clearly.

CCSS.ELA-Literacy.Writing.3.7: Conduct short research projects that build knowledge about a topic.

CCSS.ELA-Literacy.Writing.3.8: Recall information from experiences or gather information from print and digital sources; take brief notes on sources and sort evidence into provided categories.

CCSS.ELA-Literacy.Speaking/Listening.3.4: Report on a topic or text, tell a story, or recount an experience with appropriate facts and relevant, descriptive details, speaking clearly at an understandable pace.

Implementation Considerations

The "view" of the suffragette movement is broader for advanced students. Both groups are to discuss the change concept, but advanced students should focus more on how Susan B. Anthony was an exemplar of the right woman at the right time.

Differentiation Considerations

This learning experience was differentiated using grade-level concepts of the suffragette movement, but introduces:

- more advanced content to include information about how the movement began and culminated in the early 1900s;
- more complex content through the inclusion of the argument and persuasive writing aspect; and
- a focus on critical thinking by an examination of the arguments for and against the right to vote.

Assessment Considerations

Assessment should focus on the presentations of the timeline and the persuasive boards, taking into consideration the advanced content. Additionally, the persuasive pieces should recognize and rebut the arguments of the other side.

RI Standard 3 Grade 3

Grade and Standard	Typical Learners	Advanced Learners
Grade 3 RI.3.3: Describe the relationship between a series of historical events, scientific ideas or concepts, or steps in technical procedures using language related to time, sequence, and cause and effect	Read information about the arrest of Susan B. Anthony at "The Trial of Susan B. Anthony for Illegal Voting" by Doug Linder (2001). Given information about Susan B. Anthony and the suffragette movement, have students write a letter describing their feelings and their actions on November 8, 1872, the day Anthony was arrested for placing a vote in a local ballot box. Students will make a speech as if they were Susan B. Anthony demanding the right to vote (Georgia Department of Education, 2013).	Examine these materials from the National Archives: • "Appeal for a Sixteenth Amendment" from the National Woman Suffrage Association (National Archives, 2013b), and • Photo of Women Suffragettes (National Archives, 2013b). Ask students to create a visual timeline of events and the arguments used by the suffragettes to obtain the vote. Students will present arguments for and against women's voting that were present in the early 20th century. Present the arguments on mock demonstration boards.

RI Standard 3 Grade 5

Connections to Writing and Speaking/Listening

CCSS.ELA-Literacy.Writing.5.1: Write opinion pieces on topics or texts, supporting a point of view with reasons and information.

CCSS.ELA-Literacy.Writing.5.7: Conduct short research projects that use several sources to build knowledge through investigation of different aspects of a topic

CCSS.ELA-Literacy.Speaking/Listening.5.3: Summarize the points a speaker makes and explain how each claim is supported by reasons and evidence.

Interdisciplinary Connections

CCSS.Math.Content.5.NBT.A.1: Recognize that in a multidigit number, a digit in one place represents 10 times as much as it represents in the place to its right and 1/10 of what it represents in the place to its left.

Implementation Considerations

With advanced students in a small group, connections should be made between the use of zero and its complex place in history. The various puns and humor in *The Phantom Tollbooth* should be pointed out and noted, within the context of the changeability of the alphabet and the numbering system we use.

Differentiation Considerations

This learning experience was differentiated using grade-level concepts to examine the history of our alphagraphic systems, but also:
- introduces more advanced content to include the history of zero;
- increases complexity through the inclusion of the concept and functional use of zero and the question of how

math could be accomplished in historical times without it. Students will need to examine the use and process of place value; and

- focuses on critical thinking by an examination of the arguments for and against the need for zero.

Assessment Considerations

Assessment should focus on the visual presentation of the "ads" and the oral presentations of the "laws" that are persuasive in their approach. Assessments should employ elements of persuasive writing as well as presentation formats.

RI Standard 3 Grade 5

Grade and Standard	Typical Learners	Advanced Learners
Grade 5 RI.5.3: Explain the relationships or interactions between two or more individuals, events, ideas, or concepts in a historical, scientific, or technical text based on specific information in the text.	Read: • *The Phantom Tollbooth* by Norman Juster (1961/1988), and • *Ox, House, Stick: The History of our Alphabet* by Don Robb (2007). Using the relationships between the alphabetic concepts in the *Ox, House, Stick* book, the numeric concepts in *The Phantom Tollbooth*, and other specific information, have students create a commercial that attempts to persuade the residents and King of Digitopolis that letters and words are as fascinating and useful as numbers. They will use interesting stories and beautiful illustrations from the text to support your claims Students should each select a letter and research the history of that letter, sharing their story on a poster board to be made into a class book that is focused on persuading King Digitopolis that letters are interesting (Georgia Department of Education, 2013).	Read: • *The Phantom Tollbooth* by Norman Juster (1961/1988), and • *The Nothing That Is: A Natural History of Zero* by Robert Kaplan (2000). Using the relationships between the numeric concepts in the *History of Zero* book, the numeric concepts in *The Phantom Tollbooth*, and other specific information, have students create a timeline of the history of zero. Students will create a commercial that encourages the adoption of the zero and defining what zero can do for math. Advanced students will create a "law" for Digitopolis, modeled after the ancient Greek law, banning the use of zero and providing three reasons why the use of zero would create havoc. The "laws" will be presented to a "Royal Dignitary," who is to argue for the value and use of zero. Calculations should be made using Roman numerals to demonstrate the lack of zero.

RI Standard 3 Grade 8

CCSS.ELA-Literacy.Writing.8.1: Students will write arguments to support claims with clear reasons and relevant evidence.

CCSS.ELA-Literacy.Speaking/Listening.8.1c: Students will pose questions that connect the ideas of several speakers and respond to each other's questions and comments with relevant evidence, observations, and ideas.

Implementation Considerations

Prior to reading the speech by Patrick Henry, students would need some background on the situation. This could by provided by the teacher, or the teacher could ask the students to do some quick research on the occasion for Henry's speech.

The essential part of the standard here is to analyze how a text makes connections between ideas. The ideas being connected are the colonial relationship of the Americans to the British and the relationship between masters and slaves. Thus, students could do a compare and contrast analysis of how those ideas are similar and different.

Students may also require modeling and instruction on how to analyze an argument before they can analyze the argument that Henry makes in the speech. They may also need explanation of the idea of a counter-argument that could be used to refute Henry's claim.

This lesson should include group discussion, modeling of argument analysis, and participation in the Socratic seminar, in that order. Then after students have worked through the analysis as a group, the teacher might provide instruction on writing a formal argumentative paper.

Differentiation Considerations

This learning experience was differentiated using:

- greater text complexity—whereas the typical learner task is to read and analyze a news article, the gifted learners are reading and analyzing a classic text from colonial American history;
- process differentiation of analyzing the analogous relationship between being a colonist and a slave—this is a more abstract analysis than the typical analysis of the relationship or connection between people or events;
- complexity of written and oral analysis of the Socratic seminar and argumentative essay.

Assessment Considerations

Informally assess students' understanding of Henry's comparison of colonial America to that of a slave.

Assess students' participation in the Socratic seminar by evaluating their contributions to the conversation, their generation of ideas and claims, and their use of textual evidence to support their claims.

Assess students' analysis of Henry's argument and development of a counterargument to refute his claim. To do this, the teacher might use a rubric to specify elements of a counterargument that need to be used in the essay.

RI Standard 3 Grade 8

Grade and Standard	Typical Learners	Advanced Learners
Grade 8 RI.8.3 Analyze how a text makes connections among and distinctions between individuals, ideas, or events (e.g., through comparisons, analogies, or categories).	Students read a contemporary news article provided by the teacher and analyze how the author makes connections between multiple individuals, ideas, or events.	Students will read Patrick Henry's speech "Give Me Liberty or Give Me Death" (available online at http://www.history.org/almanack/life/politics/giveme.cfm) and analyze how he argues that living under British rule is analogous to a slave living under a master. Students will write a persuasive essay in which they analyze the structure of Henry's argument and refute his claim with a counterargument that it is inaccurate to characterize the rule of Britain as comparable to slavery. Students will participate in a Socratic seminar in groups of 6–10 students and share ideas of how Henry compares colonial life under Britain to slavery. Students will cite textual evidence to support their claims in the discussion.

RI Standard 3 Grades 9–10

Connection to Writing and Speaking/Listening

CCSS.ELA-Literacy.Writing.9–10.3: Write narratives to develop real or imagined experiences or events using effective technique, well-chosen details, and well-structured event sequences.

CCSS.ELA-Literacy.Speaking/Listening.9–10.1: Initiate and participate effectively in a range of collaborative discussions with diverse partners on grades 9–10 topics, texts, and issues, building on others' ideas and expressing their own clearly and persuasively.

Implementation Considerations

Prerequisites for this learning task may include background information about Theodore Roosevelt and the historical context in which he gives the speech and the communication elements of allusion and imagery as they contribute to the meaning and effectiveness of speech.

The small-group work is designed to have students collaboratively analyze Roosevelt's argument and thesis as well as his use of imagery and allusion to deepen the meaning of his ideas. Students may need guidelines on what product is expected at the conclusion of their group discussion. For instance, the students could produce a concept map or an outline of Roosevelt's argument to reflect the topics they discussed in the group.

The writing focus is self-reflective and narrative. Students need to have a clear grasp of what Roosevelt meant in his allusion to the one with the Muck-Rake and how that concept may apply to the lives of the students.

Differentiation Considerations

This learning experience was differentiated using:

- greater text complexity—Roosevelt's speech is more complex than the King letter in vocabulary and concepts; and
- process differentiation to increase the complexity of the textual analysis—students are expected to recognize Roosevelt's use of imagery and allusion in the text of his speech as tools to deepen meaning.

Assessment Considerations

Assess the students' understanding of how Roosevelt uses imagery and allusion. Assess the students' analysis of Roosevelt's thesis and argument from the group work. Focus on their skills at delineating the structure of the argument and critiquing his reasoning in support of the thesis. Use an appropriate rubric with a focus on narrative and reflective writing to assess the written products.

RI Standard 3 Grades 9–10

Grade and Standard	Typical Learners	Advanced Learners
Grades 9–10 RI.9–10.3: Analyze how the author unfolds an analysis or series of ideas or events, including the order in which the points are made, how they are introduced and developed, and the connections that are drawn between them.	Students will read Martin Luther King, Jr.'s "Letter from a Birmingham Jail" (1963/1990) and analyze how the author unfolds a series of events and develops ideas.	Students will read Theodore Roosevelt's speech "The Man With the Muck–Rake" (available at http://www.americanrhetoric.com/speeches/teddyrooseveltmuckrake.htm) and analyze how imagery and allusion are used to support Roosevelt's thesis. Students will work in small groups to discuss how Roosevelt unfolds his ideas about politics and develops his central thesis. After students have analyzed Roosevelt's speech in their small groups, they will individually write an essay analyzing a contemporary issue using Roosevelt's points made in the speech.

RI Standard 4 Grade 3

Connections to Writing and Speaking/Listening

CCSS.ELA-Literacy.Writing.3.2: Write informative/explanatory texts to examine a topic to convey ideas and information clearly.

CCSS.ELA-Literacy.Writing.3.7: Conduct short research projects that build knowledge about a topic.

CCSS.ELA-Literacy.Speaking/Listening.3.4: Report on a topic or text, tell a story, or recount an experience with appropriate facts and relevant, descriptive details, speaking clearly at an understandable pace.

Interdisciplinary Standards Connections

Science-ESS3a. Use evidence to evaluate and refine design solutions that reduce the environmental and/or societal impacts of a weather-related hazard.

Implementation Considerations

Small groups of advanced students should discuss how weather affects the global environment. Different types of weather extremes should be mapped around the globe, using the globe as a visual organizer (i.e., tsunamis in Japan, blizzards in the north, hurricanes in the south, and drought all over). Students should research and compare and contrast how different regions plan for and prepare for different emergencies. While typical students create posters and signs for a single weather incident, advanced students should examine how a single place—a school—prepares for a wide variety of weather-related issues. If the advanced students are in an inclusive setting, their products should complement the posters and products of the typical students.

Differentiation Considerations

This learning experience is differentiated using grade-level concepts of weather, but also:

- introduces more advanced content to include global information;
- adds complexity by comparing and contrasting emergency response systems in various times and places; and
- focuses on critical and creative thinking by an examination of the concept of preparedness and a realistic audience.

Assessment Considerations

Assessments should focus on the products of the Severe Weather Guide, employing the typical presentation rubric, but using advanced concepts and focusing on the complexity of a school's response to a variety of weather-related issues.

RI Standard 4 Grade 3

Grade and Standard	Typical Learners	Advanced Learners
Grade 3 RI.3.4: Determine the meanings of words and phrases in a text on a relevant topic or subject.	Read: • "Hurricanes at the Dinner Table" (Seaver, 2012), and • *I Survived Hurricane Katrina* by Lauren Tarshis (2011). After reading "Hurricanes at the Dinner Table" and *I Survived Hurricane Katrina*, implications for dress, driving, and environmental concerns for hurricanes should be drawn, using details from the reading. Hurricane and weather vocabulary words should be highlighted in the readings and explicated. Students should create posters and signs for hurricane warnings, telling citizens about what to do. Specific language related to scientific weather terms should be directly integrated.	Read: • *On the Same Day in March: A Tour of the World's Weather* by Marilyn Singer (2001), • *Night of the Twisters* by Ivy Ruckman (2003), • *Blizzard* by Jim Murphy (2000), and • A Guide to Developing a Severe Emergency Weather Plan for Schools (National Weather Service, 2002). Given information on weather around the globe, have students describe how different weather impacts precautions that locations around the world take—such as levees, dams, and specific building materials. Engage in Socratic dialogue about the preparations that different regions take for different types of weather. Students will create a Severe Emergency Weather Guide for the school, making recommendations about what types of severe weather are likely and using appropriate vocabulary. The students' Severe Emergency Weather Guide will be presented to the principal and/or the local school district.

RI Standard 4 Grade 5

Connections to Writing and Speaking/Listening

CCSS.ELA-Literacy.Writing.5.2: Write informative/explanatory texts to examine a topic and convey ideas and information clearly.

CCSS.ELA-Literacy.Writing.5.7: Conduct short research projects that use several sources to build knowledge through investigation of different aspects of a topic.

CCSS.ELA-Literacy.Speaking/Listening.5.4: Report on a topic or text or present an opinion, sequencing ideas logically and using appropriate facts and relevant, descriptive details to support main ideas or themes; speak clearly at an understandable pace.

Interdisciplinary Standards Connections

Science-PS4b: Communicate information about how technology has improved over time to increase our ability to see objects and make scientific discoveries about the universe.

Implementation Considerations

Teachers will present information from both Voyager and Curiosity, asking students to compare and contrast the different missions, purposes, formats and information. They should ask the advanced group to prepare a communication to other possible life forms about life here on Earth and what would be important to share.

Differentiation Considerations

This learning experience was differentiated using grade-level concepts of space and exploration, but also:
- more advanced content to include Voyager information;
- added complexity by comparing and contrasting what has been learned from Voyager and Curiosity; and

- focus on critical and creative thinking by a presentation of a Golden _____ to leave a message to any alien life.

Assessment Considerations

Assessment should employ a standard presentation rubric, adding components of advanced content, creativity through the use of a Golden _____, and demonstrate critical thinking through the evaluation of what is important to communicate to other life forms.

RI Standard 4 Grade 5

Grade and Standard	Typical Learners	Advanced Learners
Grade 5 RI.5.4: Determine the meaning of general academic and domain-specific words and phrases in a text relevant to a grade 5 topic or subject area.	Read: • *You Are the First Kid on Mars* by Patrick O'Brien (2009), and • Photos from Curiosity (NASA, 2013). In discussion, students will describe how Curiosity has expanded our understanding of Mars. They will plan a trip to Mars, using the guidelines suggested in *You Are the First Kid to Mars*. The plan should be presented visually, using technology.	In addition to viewing the photos from Curiosity, advanced students will read: • *Exploring the Solar System: A History With 22 Activities* (Carson, 2008), • *NASA's Voyager Missions* by Ben Evans and David Harland (2008), and • *Murmurs of Earth: The Voyager Interstellar Record* by Carl Sagan (1978). Given a history of the exploration of the solar system, students will compare and contrast the information found by Curiosity and the Voyager spacecraft using a Venn Diagram. Pose this hypothetical: "If the golden record were to be created now to leave a message for alien life on another planet, what information should be contained on it? Should it still be a record?" Students will create a presentation that details the "Golden _____" (flash drive, disk, computer, etc.) with relevant, timely information for future space intelligence. Reasons for the inclusion of certain pieces of information should be explicated.

RI Standard 4 Grade 8

Connection to Writing and Speaking Listening

- CCSS.ELA-Literacy.Writing.8.2: Write informative/explanatory texts to examine a topic and convey ideas, concepts, and information through the selection, organization, and analysis of relevant content.
- CCSS.ELA-Literacy.Speaking/Listening.8.4: Present claims and findings, emphasizing salient points in a focused, coherent manner with relevant evidence, sound valid reasoning, and well-chosen details; use appropriate eye contact, adequate volume, and clear pronunciation.

Implementation Considerations

This vocabulary development task would likely be a part of a larger unit of instruction in which the students are reading and writing. The emphasis of the task is to have students identify key words and understand their meaning and function in a complex text.

Tone may be a difficult concept for students to grasp; thus, some instruction on how authors use word choice to develop tone may be necessary.

Vocabulary webs are effective tools to develop deep understanding of words and their uses.

The purpose of the brief explanatory essay is to demonstrate that the students not only understand the meaning of the words but also how those words contribute to the author's tone in the text.

Differentiation Considerations

This learning experience was differentiated using:
- increased text complexity, and
- increased complexity in vocabulary instruction through the use of advanced words and learning activities that

require students to develop deep understandings and application of the words.

Assessment Considerations

The completion of vocabulary webs may ideally be a regularly used tool for developing vocabulary. The webs are good assessment tools to check students' understanding of words beyond basic meanings.

Assess the students' explanatory essays in a way that focuses on the use of the words to create tone.

Oral interpretations should be assessed with a rubric delineating qualities of a good performance (i.e., clarity and diction, variance in rate and volume for emphasis, etc.).

RI Standard 4 Grade 8

Grade and Standard	Typical Learners	Advanced Learners
Grade 8 RI.8.4: Determine the meaning of words and phrases as they are used in a text, including figurative, connotative, and technical meanings; analyze the impact of specific word choices on meanings and tone, including analogies or allusions to other texts.	Students will identify a news article regarding science or the environment and identify five words whose meanings are essential for the article.	Students will read Henry David Thoreau's *A Week on the Concord and Merrimack Rivers* (1849/1998). Students will identify five words whose meanings are essential for the essay. Students will develop vocabulary webs for each of the five words. Students will write a brief explanatory essay in which they explain how Thoreau uses specific words to establish his tone in the essay. Students will select a section of text which includes one or more of the key words identified from Thoreau's essay. They will give an oral interpretation (speech) of 2–3 minutes in which they present the speech to the class.

RI Standard 4 Grades 9–10

Connection to Writing and Speaking/Listening

CCSS.ELA-Literacy.Writing.9–10.2: Write informative/explanatory texts to examine and convey complex ideas, concepts, and information clearly and accurately through the effective selection, organization, and analysis of content.

CCSS.ELA-Literacy.Speaking/Listening.9–10.4: Present information, findings, and supporting evidence clearly, concisely, and logically such that listeners can follow the line of reasoning, and the organization, development, substance, and style are appropriate to purpose, audience, and task.

Implementation Considerations

Although the text of Epicurus' letter is short, it includes a complex argument. There would likely be several learning goals in this project, including vocabulary, textual analysis, critique of an argument, developing writing skills, and developing speaking skills in the context of a debate.

For the purposes of this standard, the vocabulary focus is on understanding the meaning and impact of words and phrases in the text. The teacher may want to identify the key words and phrases for analysis or may let the students select them. The teacher may also use both teacher-selected and student-selected words.

Vocabulary webs are an evidence-supported practice that helps students build understandings of words and phrases.

The essay and debate are connections to the writing and speaking/listening standards and will reinforce students' overall comprehension of the text including the key words and phrases that have been studied.

Differentiation Considerations

This learning experience was differentiated using:

- text complexity,
- advanced content through more advanced vocabulary in the text of the Epicurus letter than in a typical grade-level assigned text, and
- complexity of the concepts and ideas being written about and debated.

Assessment Considerations

Assess student understanding of the key terms and phrases. For instance, the teacher may use the students' vocabulary webs as evidence of understanding, but she may also expect students to demonstrate their understanding of the terms and phrases in speaking and writing.

Assess the writing with an appropriate and rigorous rubric for informative writing.

A rubric should be developed and used to clarify the expectations for the debate. It is recommended to use a formal debate format with 3–4-minute affirmative and negative speeches as well as rebuttal speeches for each. Questioning the speaker is also a potential step in the debate process that allows students to clarify meaning and speaking skills.

RI Standard 4 Grades 9–10

Grade and Standard	Typical Learners	Advanced Learners
Grades 9–10 RI.9–10.4: Determine the meaning of words and phrases as they are used in a text, including figurative, connotative, and technical meanings; analyze the cumulative impact of specific word choices on meaning and tone.	Students will select and read a news story on a current event in science or ethics and write a summary of the text while also identifying five vocabulary words on which to create vocabulary webs.	Students will read Epicurus' "Letter to Menoeceus" (available at http://classics.mit.edu/Epicurus/menoec.html) and identify what they believe to be the most important terms and phrases Epicurus uses in the letter. Students will create vocabulary webs to develop understanding and impact of the words and phrases. Students will write an informative essay in which they explain Epicurus' use of the important term or phrase, and the impact the term or phrase has on the overall meaning and interpretation of the text. Students will participate in a debate in teams of two in which they debate Epicurus' perspective on the role of pleasure in life.

RI Standard 9 Grade 3

Connections to Writing and Speaking/Listening

CCSS.ELA-Literacy.Writing.3.2: Write informative/explanatory texts to examine a topic to convey ideas and information clearly.

CCSS.ELA-Literacy.Writing.3.7: Conduct short research projects that build knowledge about a topic.

Implementation Considerations

Teachers will ask advanced students to look at how activism and stories impact global issues. By examining not just the stories of individual children, but conferences designed to focus on children's issues, they can understand the global issues that impact children around the world.

Differentiation Considerations

This activity was differentiated using grade-level concepts of human rights, but also:

- introduces more advanced content through the expanded global issues of child soldiers and global warming;
- adds complexity in evaluating which issues would be most worthy of a conference and synthesizing the information into session descriptions; and
- focuses on critical and creative thinking by the design of a conference.

Assessment Considerations

Typical rubrics for summarization statements should be used for advanced learners, adding in aspects of global understanding and more advanced content. The rubric for the persuasive piece should focus on the use of persuasive elements for a specific purpose, or the use of comparing and contrasting techniques for the purpose of persuasion.

RI Standard 9 Grade 3

Grade and Standard	Typical Learners	Advanced Learners
Grade 3 RI.3.9: Compare and contrast the most important points and key details presented in two texts on the same topic	Read the information on these sites: • Universal Declaration of Human Rights: http://www.un.org/en/documents/udhr/index.shtml • Universal Declaration of Human Rights, Plain Language Version: http://www.un.org/cyberschoolbus/humanrights/resources/plain.asp • Stories of Human Rights for Children: http://www.un.org/cyberschoolbus/humanrights/stories.asp Guide students in exploring the stories of the children posted on this site (they are short, original, and illustrate how very different the lives of impoverished or oppressed people around the world can be from our own lives). They will write synopses of the statements for inclusion in a theoretical conference of children, for children. Allow the students to explore the stories, making notes on a T-chart that compares and contrasts the most important points and key details between their lives and those of the students in the stories.	Read the information on these sites: • UN Student Conference on Human Rights: http://gem-ngo.org/UN-Day.html • Child Soldiers International: http://www.child-soldiers.org Students will create their version of the UN Student Conference on Human Rights. They will research the programs from the years past, and the various topics that have been discussed. Students will organize a program for a conference next year that addresses at least six topics and four potential speakers. Each issue should relate to a particular concern or event in the world today, such as child soldiers in Sierra Leone and other parts of Africa. Students will write conference session "descriptions" of what the content of the session is going to be. After researching the global issues, students will brainstorm a list of possible topics and concerns. Advanced students will write an advocacy paper addressing one of the issues for presentation to a selected service organization in the school.

RI Standard 9 Grade 5

Connections to Writing and Speaking/Listening

CCSS.ELA-Literacy.Writing.5.1: Write opinion pieces on topics or texts, supporting a point of view with reasons and information.

CCSS.ELA-Literacy.Writing.5.7: Conduct short research projects that use several sources to build knowledge through investigation of different aspects of a topic.

Implementation Considerations

Teachers should focus not just on the existence of the Code Talkers, but also on their role in keeping the Navajo culture alive after government activities to eradicate it. There could be some significant discussion about what it is to be "American" and how the Navajo, despite having a different language, are American as well.

Differentiation Considerations

This activity was differentiated using grade-level concepts of human rights and cultural capital, but also:

- introduces more advanced content to include the complicated role between the federal government and the use of the Native American languages;
- adds complexity by drawing inferences between the practice of the government and the value of the "foreign" language; and
- focuses on critical and creative thinking through a presentation of the relationship between language, cultural value, and cultural capital.

Assessment Considerations

Assessment should focus on the use of data within a persuasive framework. A persuasive writing rubric should be employed to assess the level of critical thinking.

RI Standard 9 Grade 5

Grade and Standard	Typical Learners	Advanced Learners

Grade 5
RI.5.9: Integrate information from several texts on the same topic in order to write or speak about the subject knowledgeably.
	Read:
	• "Creating the Code" (Allen, 2012), and
	• *Code Talkers: A Novel About the Navajo Marines of World War Two* by Joseph Bruchac (2006).
	
	In the book, following Code Talker training completion, Ned and his fellow Navajos translated the "Marine Corp Hymn" into the Navajo language. Since many English words do not translate directly to Navajo, the two versions are different. At the end of Chapter 12, Ned explains the meaning of the Navajo translation.
	    Students will discuss how this meaning captures the Navajo concepts, yet still remains "American."
	    Using the novel and the resources found at http://www.youtube.com/watch?v=SwS6Ok gUXKE&feature=related and http://www.scoutsongs.com/lyrics/marinecorpshymn.html, students will write an essay comparing and contrasting the meanings of the two versions.
		Read:
		• "WWII pigeon message stumps GCHQ decoders" by Gordon Corera (2012),
		• *Code Talker: The First and Only Memoir by One of the Original Navajo Code Talkers of WWII* (Nez & Avila, 2012),
		• Memo From Commander General Vogel Regarding Enlistment of Navajo Indians (National Archives, 2013a), and
		• Information About Carlisle Indian Industrial School (Landis, 2001).
		
		Students will discuss the memo from Commander Vogel in which he discusses the fact that there were only 28 speakers in the entire country who were strong enough speakers to create the code and discuss why they think there were only 28.
		    Ask students to research the practices of forced cultural assimilation, such as the Carlisle Indian Industrial School's practices of eradicating the native language. How did the Navajo Code Talkers help keep the value of their native language alive?
		    Students should argue their opinion about whether the Navajo Code Talkers helped keep the Navajo culture alive.

RI Standard 9 Grade 8

Connection to Writing and Speaking/Listening

CCSS.ELA-Literacy.Writing.8.1: Write arguments to support claims with clear reasons and relevant evidence.

CCSS.ELA-Literacy.Speaking/Listening.8.4: Present claims and findings emphasizing salient points in a focused, coherent manner with relevant evidence, sound, valid reasoning, and well-chosen details; use appropriate eye contact, adequate volume, and clear pronunciation.

Implementation Considerations

As the students read these texts, they should develop a web or outline of the ideas and arguments presented.

The Declaration of Independence is the base text for the comparison. Students will compare the King and Smith texts to the concepts of freedom and independence in the Declaration of Independence. Thus, first and foremost, students must analyze what the Declaration says about freedom and independence.

The second level of analysis is to analyze what King is saying about freedom and independence. The third level of analysis is to analyze what Smith is saying about freedom and independence. The final level of analysis is for students to look for similarities and differences in the ways that King and Smith argue that freedom and independence, in reality, are not as clearly established and maintained as declared in the Declaration of Independence.

To write and deliver the argumentative speech, the students must identify a position that is derived from their analysis of King and Smith's speeches with relation to the Declaration of Independence.

Differentiation Considerations

This learning experience was differentiated using:

- greater text complexity—the three documents that are being analyzed and compared are significant primary texts with complex ideas and sophisticated language and vocabulary;
- an emphasis on conceptual understanding of the concepts of freedom and independence; and
- a focus on critical thinking, as students have to analyze arguments of three complex texts and then engage in comparative analysis.

Assessment Considerations

Assess students' analyses of the theses and arguments being presented in all three texts (critical-thinking skills). Students need to demonstrate a solid grasp of main ideas and supporting details. Assess students' comparison of the King and Smith texts to the Declaration of Independence. For the written assignment, use an appropriate rubric to assess persuasive writing. For the speeches, use a rubric designed to measure characteristics of a quality speech.

RI Standard 9 Grade 8

Grade and Standard	Typical Learners	Advanced Learners
Grade 8 RI.8.9. Analyze a case in which two or more texts provide conflicting information on the same topic and identify where the texts disagree on matters of fact or interpretation.	Students will read contradictory accounts in two texts of a current event in the news and analyze how the two authors vary in their view of the facts and the interpretation of the events.	Students will read The Declaration of Independence, "I Have a Dream" by Martin Luther King, Jr. (1963/1990), and Margaret Chase Smith's "Remarks to the Senate in Support of a Declaration of Conscience" (http://www.senate.gov/artandhistory/history/resources/pdf/SmithDeclaration.pdf). Students will analyze how King and Smith challenge existence of freedom and independence as articulated by the writers of the Declaration. Students will write argumentative speeches in which they take a position and defend it on the concept of either freedom or independence. They will include text evidence from all three texts in their speeches. Students will deliver argumentative speeches based on the speeches they wrote. Furthermore, students in the class will pose questions to the speakers connecting the ideas between speakers and texts.

RI Standard 9 Grades 9–10

Connection to Writing and Speaking/Listening

CCSS.ELA-Literacy.Writing.9–10.7: Conduct short as well as more sustained research projects to answer a question or solve a problem; narrow or broaden the inquiry when appropriate; synthesize multiple sources on the subject, demonstrating understanding of the subject under investigation.

CCSS.ELA-Literacy.Speaking/Listening.9–10.4: Present information, findings, and supporting evidence clearly, concisely, and logically such that listeners can follow the line of reasoning and the organization, development, and style are appropriate to purpose, audience, and task.

Implementation Considerations

In order to develop a clear understanding of the texts, students should utilize a close reading strategy, such as Cornell notes, a concept map, or a detailed outline.

Class discussion over the texts should focus on the situations in which Washington and Hand gave their speeches and the main ideas communicated. As students answer questions about the text during discussion, focus the conversation on the concept of patriotism. Ask the students to generate ideas about how the two texts define or describe patriotism.

During the small-group research process, students may be required to find three to five additional speeches that deal with the subject of patriotism in American history. Because the analysis involves noting changes over time in the concept of patriotism, it would be important for students to find speeches from various points in time between the Washington speech and the present.

Oral commentaries ask students to make speeches in an impromptu fashion over short selections of text.

Differentiation Considerations

This learning experience was differentiated using:
- greater text difficulty—students engage in comparative analyses;
- conceptual understanding of an abstract concept as it changes over time; and
- advanced skills in oral commentary demand (which may be adjusted by the amount of time students are expected to speak on the selected text).

Assessment Considerations

Potential items to consider in assessment of the research component include evaluation of appropriateness of sources, analysis of each source, and synthesis of ideas across multiple sources. Additionally, assess the group presentation on required elements including the following: clearly stated thesis, valid reasoning to defend the thesis, and references to primary sources to support the reasoning.

Assess students' understanding of the concept of patriotism including the subtle differences between Washington and Hand.

The oral commentary is a technique to assess students' ability to speak from a solid understanding of a particular text. The students are aware that the teacher will select a segment of text from one of the two speeches, but they don't know which segment. Once the student receives his or her segment from the teacher, he or she has five minutes to make a few notes before standing in front of the group to give an analysis speech over the selected text. Generally the oral commentaries are limited to no more than 10 minutes. Younger or more inexperienced students may be asked to speak for 3 or 4 minutes and build up to longer commentaries with experience. Assess students according to the standards of clarity and quality in the speaking and listening standards by developing an appropriate rubric.

RI Standard 9 Grades 9–10

Grade and Standard	Typical Learners	Advanced Learners
Grades 9–10 RI.9–10.9: Analyze seminal U.S. documents of historical and literary significance, including how they address related themes and concepts.	Students will read George Washington's "Farewell Address" (http://avalon.law.yale.edu/18th_century/washing.asp) and create a graphic organizer to illustrate Washington's main ideas stated in their own words.	Students will read George Washington's "Farewell Address" and Judge Learned Hand's "I Am an American Day" address (http://www.providence-forum.org/spiritoflibertyspeech) and compare and contrast how they treat the concept of patriotism. Students will work in small groups of 3–5 to research primary documents (i.e., speeches) in American history with the guiding question: How has the concept of patriotism changed over time from George Washington to the present? The research project would be a combination of in–class and outside-of-class work over a period of about 2 weeks. The result of the research would be a 7–10-minute group presentation in which the group presents a thesis and defends it with evidence from the primary sources that they found in the research. Students will give oral commentaries over passages from either Washington's or Hand's speeches.

Differentiating Assessments to Develop English Language Arts Talent

The CCSS–ELA articulate the grade-level standards of performance for all students. These standards provide a valuable tool for educators to focus on the content of the discipline and the habits of professionals in the discipline (VanTassel-Baska, 2003). Standards such as the CCSS–ELA also become a starting point or a springboard for differentiation for gifted learners (Tomlinson, 1999) and a roadmap for the development of expertise and talent. As part of the talent development process, language arts educators should provide differentiated learning experiences and appropriate assessments adapted for the advanced abilities of students gifted in the language arts (Stambaugh, 2011).

In this guide, assessment considerations have been addressed for each of the examples. Assessment considerations describe the processes or products on which the students ought to be assessed in the instructional example. In some cases, the assessment considerations are formative, and in other cases, they are summative. Both should be used regularly to provide feedback to students during the learning and at the culmination of the instructional unit. Process skills may include participation in discussions or working with groups (which addresses the speaking and listening standards), and final products (which addresses the writing standards) may include typical written products as well as performances such as speeches and multimedia presentations. The assessment considerations in these examples recommend that teachers focus assessment on conceptual understandings, higher level thinking, and advanced content knowledge. Although specific rubrics for assessment are not included with the examples, the use of well-developed rubrics is recommended (see p. 147).

Assessment should play a critical role in developing language arts talent, but in order to do so, it must be adapted to reflect the advanced abilities of students and the content and processes of differentiated curriculum. Assessments should take multiple forms to accomplish formative and summative feedback goals and foster increasingly advanced levels of student performance. First, standardized assessments are being developed to measure student mastery of the grade-level core standards. Educators of the gifted need to understand the format and expectations for those standardized assessments (see http://www.smarterbalanced. org and http://www.parcconline.org). Additionally, educators of the gifted should develop classroom assessments for students with items similar to those being developed for standardized CCSS-ELA assessments while differentiating the complexity of the texts students read for the corresponding items. Four archetypal assessment formats have been articulated (Measured Progress/ETS Collaborative, 2012) to provide multiple formats for assessing language arts performance claims (see Figure 1). Second, authentic assessments developed by teachers or teams of teachers should be differentiated according to the advanced language arts competencies in gifted students. These authentic assessments may be performance-based or product-based. Rubrics should be developed or differentiated that measure student performance on advanced learning tasks. Furthermore, these rubrics should be developed with advanced performance indicators to eliminate ceiling effects common with gifted student assessment. For example, rubrics on which gifted students readily and consistently score in the highest category are not

Element	0: Poor	1: Acceptable	2: Good	3: Exemplary
Use of Advanced Content	No advanced content integrated into product.	Some advanced material present with integration into the product.	Advanced material present and well integrated into product.	Significant quantity and quality of advanced materials integrated into products.
Critical Thinking	Insights are shallow or reflect only surface-level understanding.	Insights are reflective and make connections with content.	Insights are in-depth and connect content in thoughtful and thorough manners.	Insights add considerably to the understanding of a piece and provide new learnings and new understandings.
Depth	Products reflect only single-level or surface-level understanding. There are no or insufficient connections to other ideas and/or content.	Products reflect multiple levels of understanding. There are some relevant connections to other ideas and content.	Products reflect understanding of the concept and how it relates to other concepts. Sufficient and insightful connections to other ideas are made.	Significantly insightful connections to other ideas, concepts, and/or content is made. Ideas are explored and boundaries of understanding defined.
Creative Thinking	Products or ideas are similar to those of other students and do not demonstrate an elaborated response.	Products or ideas reflect some individuality and elaboration beyond the ordinary.	Products or ideas are innovative and reflect significant individuality.	Products or ideas are advanced, unique, and innovative.

Figure 1. Assessment rubric for gifted and advanced learners.

effective tools for eliciting student growth or delineating variance in advanced levels of performance. In addition to state-required or school-provided grade-level rubrics for typical learners, we recommend that the following components be added to rubrics for gifted and advanced learners.

Differentiating Classroom Assessments

As demonstrated in this guide and previous guides for differentiating the CCSS for gifted students (Johnsen & Sheffield, 2013; VanTassel-Baska, 2013), differentiation for gifted or advanced students can be accomplished in multiple ways. In some cases, acceleration strategies increase the pace at which students master the curriculum and result in students working on above-grade-level learning outcomes. In other cases, the curriculum is differentiated through the addition of elements of depth and complexity. Differentiation may also include a greater emphasis on critical thinking, creative thinking, or problem solving. Content differentiation through the use of above-grade-level texts is one particular way that the curriculum should be differentiated in the CCSS-ELA for reading literature and reading informational texts. The examples in this guide frequently include above-grade-level texts for reading even though the learning tasks also include enrichment of the grade-level standards.

Teachers can differentiate for gifted students by increasing text complexity while assessing the same grade-level standards for all students. For instance, based on the current CCSS-ELA assessment resources (see http://www.smarterbalanced.org and http://www.parcconline.org), the following reading literature and informational text standards will be assessed:

- Read closely to determine what the text says explicitly and to make logical inferences from it; cite specific textual evidence when writing or speaking to support conclusions drawn from the text (ELA Anchor Standard 1).
- Determine central ideas or themes from a text and analyze their development; summarize the key supporting details and ideas (ELA Anchor Standard 2).

All students should be assessed on their ability to transfer and apply these skills on a selection of text that they have not yet read or studied. The differentiated element is the selection of text at a higher reading and complexity level for gifted students. Teachers or teams of teachers should develop and use a variety of assessment items in all four of the archetypal formats: selected response, constructed response, performance tasks, and technology-enhanced (see Table 1). Assessing all students' mastery of the CCSS-ELA should employ these four assessment types, but differentiation for gifted learners often requires using different texts. In some cases, the assessment item stems could be the same, but the possible responses would vary based on the text.

Differentiating Selected Response Items. For example, an eighth-grade language arts class concludes a unit on poetry. Throughout the unit, the teacher differentiated learning experiences by having gifted students read above-grade-level poetry texts. The learning objective of the unit was RL.8.1: *Cite the textual evidence that most strongly supports an analysis of what the text says explicitly as well as inferences drawn from the text.* To assess students' mastery of this learning outcome, the teacher decided to create an assessment consisting of selected response items similar to what is expected on the state assessment. Students were given a text that they have not previously read or studied. The typical eighth-grade students were given "The Road Not Taken" by Robert Frost. The advanced eighth-grade students, who had differentiated experiences during the unit, were given "We Must Grow Accustomed to the Dark" by Emily Dickinson, a text exemplar for typical high school students. Selected response item stems common to both typical and advanced students included the following:

1. Which of the following phrases from the poem best supports the author's theme?
2. Which of the following phrases from the poem best reveals the author's use of irony?
3. Which of the following phrases suggests the author had both a literal and an inferential meaning?

Table 1.

Archetypal Assessment Item Formats

Item Type	Description
Selected Response (SR)	Selected response items are multiple-choice items. They should include three or more answer choices. All choices should be of similar length and format. All choices should be plausible and there must be a correct or best answer.
Constructed Response (CR)	Constructed response items require students to write a brief response to a prompt. CR items measure students' ability to think and reason and use higher order skills. CR items relate to a stimulus (text or audio/visual) and students respond to the items based on the stimulus. CR items must include a rubric for scoring student responses; CCSS-ELA assessments will likely present CR items that are scored on a two- or three-point rubric.
Performance Task (PT)	Performance task items require students to read and write full texts or speeches in response to the texts they read. PT items measure analytical thinking and evaluation. The number and complexity of the texts for PT will increase across grade levels from one to five texts. Texts could be audio/visual as well as textual. With multiple texts, the task complexity generally increases. PT items must include a rubric that is more detailed and generally has a wider score range. PT scoring rubrics may include up to 20 points.
Technology Enhanced (TE)	Technology-enhanced items include the use of technology and can be useful to measure students' skills that are not easily measured in SR, CR, or PT items. For instance, TE items could require students to edit a text selection or require students to highlight text that supports a claim or contextually defines a term. TE items may embed video to measure listening skills or a source of text to which students write responses.

4.   Which of the following might be inferred from the poem?
5.   What might be inferred from the author's choice of title?

Additional selected response items would be specific to the stimulus text, either Frost or Dickinson.

Differentiating Constructed Response Items. A fifth-grade teacher had students read informational texts about Presidents Day. Purpose-setting questions leading up to the reading included: Why do we celebrate Presidents Day? When did it begin? Which president or presidents are we celebrating? After the initial discussions, the teacher assigned differentiated texts for the students to read. Typical students read an article from *Time for Kids*, "Presidents' Day Dilemma" (Time for Kids, 2013). Advanced readers read a similar article from *Time*, "A Brief History of (What You Think Is) Presidents' Day" (Newcomb, 2012). In this learning task, all students read informational texts about Presidents Day, but the text was differentiated, requiring advanced readers to read a text with more advanced vocabulary and more complex ideas. The CCSS-ELA standard that the teacher taught and assessed was RI.5.2: *Determine two or more main ideas of a text and explain how they are supported by details; summarize the text*. To focus assessment on students' understanding of main idea, the teacher decided to create constructed response items. Some of the constructed response item stems might be common to both groups—the typical readers and the advanced readers. For instance, both groups would construct responses to the following:

1. Describe the author's main idea in the text.
2. Write another possible title for this text and explain why it is appropriate.
3. Identify a claim for which the author might not have provided enough support and suggest one or two sentences that would better support his claim.

In addition to the common constructed response item stems, each group might have one or more text-particular constructed response items such as the following for advanced readers: The author claims that the purpose of Presidents Day is confused. Provide textual evidence from the news article that supports this claim.

Each of these four constructed response items would include concise, two-point rubrics to measure student responses on a scale of zero, one, or two points earned. Ideally, teachers or teams of teachers would develop these two-point rubrics to accompany a battery of constructed response item stems that could accompany any text.

In both of the reading examples above, the teacher differentiated the assessment by providing an above-grade-level, more complex text for the gifted students. The item stems on the selected response and constructed response assessments may be the same for both groups of students (typical and advanced readers). All of the items measure mastery of the grade-level standards for reading literature (RL.8.1) or reading informational texts (RI.5.2), but the learning task and the assessment were differentiated for gifted learners with above-grade-level texts. Further differentiation of the constructed response items could include differentiated two-point rubrics for the advanced reader responses. Both examples demonstrate that teachers can differentiate assessments while at the same time measuring student performance on grade-level standards. Advanced students are more likely to grow in reading ability through the reading of above-grade-level texts, and the teacher can feel confident that preparation for required state assessments does not restrict appropriate differentiation.

Differentiating Performance Task Items. Performance task assessment items are generally used to assess students' writing and thinking skills. Similar to the way that the selected response items and the constructed response assessments can be differentiated, performance task assessments can be differentiated through the use of more complex texts. When using performance task items, teachers provide students with one or more texts to read followed by a performance task. It is typical that constructed response items accompany performance task items (Measured Progress/ETS Collaborative, 2012). A typical performance task assessment might last approximately 2 hours broken into two parts. In the first part, the students read the texts provided and respond to two or three constructed response items. These constructed response items serve a specific prewriting function to honor the planning process of quality writing. In the second part, the students write a full-length essay in response to the prompt.

For example, a 10th-grade English teacher had a class of typical and advanced students. The class has been studying the rhetoric of argumentative writing based on the CCSS-ELA W9–10.1: *Write arguments to support claims in an analysis of substantive topics or texts, using valid reasoning and sufficient evidence.* The teacher develops a performance task assessment to measure the progress and mastery of the skills being taught in the instructional unit. To differentiate the performance task, the teacher selects differentiated texts to use as the stimulus for the argumentative essay. For the typical students, she locates two news articles on the role of the Ten Commandments in schools. For a third article, she selects a section from the Anti-Defamation League's (2012) paper, "The Ten Commandments in the Public Square." For the advanced learners, she selects two paragraphs from Richard Rorty's (1990) essay, "The Priority of Democracy to Philosophy," an excerpt from Thomas Jefferson's (1786) "The Virginia Act for Establishing Religious Freedom," and the First Amendment to the Constitution of the United States of America. For both groups of students, the texts focus on the same issue—establishment of religion in a democracy. However, the text difficulty is more complex for the advanced learners.

The differentiated performance task assessment for both groups includes three constructed response items to serve as prewriting for the full essay:

1. Describe the main idea common to all three of the texts.
2. Identify three claims made regarding religion in schools.
3. From any one of the three texts, restate the main claim and summarize the authors' justification of the claim.

Students would be allowed roughly 40 minutes for Part I and roughly 80 minutes for Part II of the assessment. For the second part of the performance task, the students are asked to write an argumentative essay including textual evidence. Specifically, the students are asked to make a claim regarding the role of religion in schools and rationally defend their position. For assessing the students' responses, two-point rubrics would be used for the three constructed responses. For assessing the full essay, a detailed argumentative essay rubric would be used. The assessment task is differentiated through the use of more complex texts. For a more advanced level of differentiation, the teacher might also use differentiated rubrics for the constructed responses and the argumentative essay.

Differentiating Technology Enhanced Items. Technology enhanced items can assess a range of learning targets. Technology-enhanced items might include embedded video to measure listening skills, such as the College and Career Readiness Anchor (CCRA) SL.3: *Evaluate a speaker's point of view, reasoning, and use of evidence and rhetoric.* Technology-enhanced items could also be used to measure CCRA.RI.4: *Interpret words and phrases as they are used in text, including determining technical, connotative, and figurative meanings, and analyze how specific word choices shape meaning and tone.* The following example illustrates how a teacher might use technology-enhanced items to assess student progress or mastery in the language standards.

A fourth-grade teacher has been teaching writing skills and conventions to her class that includes both typical and advanced students. To assess students' skills in language, she decides to develop a technology-enhanced assessment. Specifically, her assessment focuses on the following CCSS-ELA language standards: L.4.1: *Demonstrate command of the conventions of standard English grammar and usage when writing or speaking*; and L.4.2: *Demonstrate command of the standard English capitalization, punctuation, and spelling when writing.* In this situation, the teacher is going to provide students with a selection of text in a Microsoft Word document. The technology-enhanced item asks them to revise and edit the document to reflect standard English grammar and usage, capitalization, punctuation, and spelling. For her typical students, the teacher finds a selection of text from the grade-level science resources. When she creates the text sample for the assignment, she alters the text to include a number of errors in need of editing and revision. For the advanced students, the teacher finds a selection of text from the website http://scienceblogs.com. Similar to the text for typical students, the teacher creates a text sample for the advanced learner assignment in which she alters the text to include a number of errors in need of editing and revision. The differentiated text includes more sophisticated language and more difficult editing and revision tasks because the vocabulary, spelling, and sentence structures are more advanced. To complete the technology-enhanced assessment, the students either work in a technology lab or with a classroom set of computers. A benefit of technology-enhanced assessment items is the development of college and career technology skills while also assessing revising and editing skills. Thus, the teacher may need to teach the students how to use the track changes feature of Microsoft Word as part of the instructional unit and assessment.

Differentiating Authentic Assessments

Authentic assessments have been advocated as appropriate tools for assessing gifted students' knowledge and skills in all domains including language arts (Moon, Brighton, Callahan, & Robinson, 2005; VanTassel-Baska, 2008a). Authentic assessments articulate standards of performance that are expected on open-ended learning tasks. Advanced authentic assessments for gifted students should focus on higher levels of skills, including application, analysis, synthesis, and evaluation. In a differentiated language arts program, gifted students should read above-grade-level texts, and complete more challenging, open-ended assignments including writing and presenting.

A differentiated approach to curriculum and instruction provides advanced learning experiences and rigorous assignments. A differentiated approach to assessing rigorous assignments requires assessment rubrics that specify advanced levels of performance. A teacher or teams of teachers may design rubrics, or they may select rubrics from external resource providers. The challenge is to find or develop rubrics that articulate advanced levels of performance, commensurate with expectations for gifted students. Advanced rubrics in language arts should measure the following dimensions of performance tasks: advanced writing skills, analysis and interpretation of text, conceptual understanding, creative thinking, and critical thinking.

In addition to advanced rubrics that measure knowledge and skills, assessments should also provide qualitative data on students' reflections of their performances. Questions to guide students' reflection on their own work might include:

1. In what ways is this work an improvement over my last work?
2. What are the strengths of this work?
3. In what ways might I improve this work in the future?

Teachers should use a rubric to assess the students' self-assessment (see Table 2). The rubric serves not only as an assessment tool, but also as a guide to help students understand what good and exemplary self-reflection looks like. Well-designed rubrics become both measures of and tools for learning.

Ideally, teachers, schools, and districts would develop a battery of assessment rubrics that articulate performance to meet the standard, as well as performance that is above the standard and performance that is exemplary. High-quality rubrics are a necessary complement to differentiated, advanced learning tasks. However, high-quality rubrics should be tested for validity and reliability. Users of the rubrics should have training opportunities to improve their understanding of student work that meets the standard, exceeds the standard, and significantly exceeds the standard. A differentiated rubric should articulate multiple levels of advanced performance with the highest category reserved for truly outstanding achievement. If gifted students consistently perform at the highest level of the rubric, it is not sufficiently differentiated. A well-differentiated rubric not only allows teachers to accurately assess high levels of performance, but it also allows students to see areas for growth (see Table 3).

In a systematically differentiated school or school district, advanced rubrics would be developed and aligned for specific areas across grade-level bands. Regular opportunities for training would be available to teachers to understand the components of

Table 2.
Teacher Assessment of Student Self-Assessment

	0: Poor	1: Acceptable	2: Good	3: Exemplary
Improvement Over Previous Work	Student does not identify elements of the current work that are improvements from previous work.	Student identifies some elements of the current work that are improvements from previous work.	Student identifies some elements of the current work that are improvements from previous work and explains the difference.	Student identifies several elements of the current work that are improvements from previous work and justifies why the current elements are superior to similar elements in the previous work.
Strengths of This Work	Student does not describe any strengths of the current work.	Student identifies a few strengths of the current work.	Student identifies a few strengths of the current work and justifies why these features are considered strengths.	Student identifies several strengths of the current work and justifies why these features are considered strengths.
Ways to Improve in the Future	Student does not identify any ways that the work could be improved in the future.	Student identifies a few ways that the work could be improved in the future.	Student identifies a few ways that the work could be improved in the future and gives examples.	Student identifies several ways the work could be improved in the future and gives examples for each.

Table 3.

Format for Differentiated Rubrics

	Below Standard	Average	Good	Very Good	Exemplary
Description	Work does not meet the grade-level standard.	Work that meets the grade-level standard.	Work exceeds the grade-level standard.	Work that exceeds the differentiated standard.	Reserved for rare occasions of truly outstanding achievement.
Prevalence	Small percentage of gifted student work that is unacceptable. 5%–10%	Small percentage of gifted student work that does not exceed grade-level standards. 10%–20%	Majority of gifted student work. 50%–70%	Small percentage of gifted student work that is beyond even the differentiated standard. Top 10%–20%	Extremely small percentage of work that is extraordinary. Top 1%–5%

advanced achievement and how they can be assessed. Ideally the rubrics and the training result in teachers consistently agreeing on how to score student products (interrater reliability) and students clearly understanding what knowledge and skills are required for advanced levels of performance (validity). A well-developed battery of assessment rubrics for the CCSS-ELA would include graduated rubrics aligned to the scope and sequence of the standards (see Table 4). In the graduated system, students across a band of grade levels would use the same rubric each time they work on a specific product (e.g., informative writing). The consistency of the rubric creates a unified understanding of quality indicators for both students and teachers. The complexity of the rubric would increase gradually across grade-level bands.

Implementation of the CCSS-ELA for gifted students requires careful consideration of differentiation in curriculum, instruction, and assessment based on the characteristics of gifted learners in the language arts domain. To focus only on the curriculum and instruction without also differentiating assessment leads to poor alignment and inconsistency between stated and measured objectives. Furthermore, quality differentiated assess-

Table 4.

Sample Battery of Rubrics for Differentiated Language Arts

Area	Specific Content Rubrics	Graduated Sequence of Rubrics
Reading	• Literary Text Analysis • Informational Text Analysis	• Kindergarten • Grades 1–2 • Grades 3–5 • Grades 6–8 • Grades 9–10 • Grades 11–12
Writing	• Argumentative Writing • Informative Writing • Narrative Writing	• Kindergarten • Grades 1–2 • Grades 3–5 • Grades 6–8 • Grades 9–10 • Grades 11–12
Speaking and Listening	• Oral Presentations • Multimedia Presentations • Group Participation	• Kindergarten • Grades 1–2 • Grades 3–5 • Grades 6–8 • Grades 9–10 • Grades 11–12
Learning Process	• Self-Reflection • Peer Evaluation • Independent Study • Research Processes	• Kindergarten–Grade 2 • Grades 3–5 • Grades 6–8 • Grades 9–12

ments have been found to promote advanced levels of student learning (VanTassel-Baska & Stambaugh, 2008). Differentiated assessments provide valid feedback for gifted students as they traverse the language arts talent development trajectory, and such feedback is a necessary component to continual progress along the continuum. In a comprehensive system of differentiated assessment, teachers would differentiate classroom assessments when using the archetypal assessment items. This is specifically accomplished through the differentiation of the text used as part of the assessment. Additionally, a comprehensive system of differentiated assessments would include a battery of high-quality rubrics that both assess and guide advanced levels of performance for gifted students (see Table 5).

Table 5.
Rubrics and Resources for Assessment

Rubrics Needed For Examples	Resources for Construction/Adaptation
Debate	William & Mary Language Arts Units (http://education.wm.edu/centers/cfge) Association for the Assessment of Learning in Higher Education (AALHE) Assessment Resources (http://course1.winona.edu/shatfield/air/rubrics.htm)
Advanced Products	Texas Performance Standards Project (http://www.texaspsp.org)
Speaking and Listening	Oral Presentation Rubric from ReadWriteThink.org (http://www.readwritethink.org)
Analyzing Literature	Partnership for Assessment of Readiness for College and Careers (http://www.parcconline.org) Smarter Balanced Assessments (http://www.smarterbalanced.org) Poetry Out Loud Scoring Rubric (http://www.poetryoutloud.org)
Persuasive Writing	Persuasive Writing Scoring Guide from ReadWriteThink.org (http://www.readwritethink.org) Smarter Balanced Assessments (http://www.smarterbalanced.org)
Expository Writing	Great Books Foundation Assessment Tools (http://www.greatbooks.org)
Grammar and Usage	*Using the Common Core for English Language Arts with Gifted and Advanced Learners* (http://www.nagc.org) National Writing Project Resources (http://www.nwp.org)
Text-Based Discussion	Great Books Foundation Critical Thinking Rubric (http://www.greatbooks.org)

Resources to Assist With English Language Arts Differentiation

There are a variety of resources that can assist university personnel, administrators, and coordinators of gifted programs at state and local levels in differentiating instruction in English language arts in order to implement the new CCSS-ELA for gifted learners. A range of resources is provided below related to English language arts associations, assessment tools, differentiated and research-based curriculum units, and instructional strategies that employ the use of higher order thinking skills.

The NAGC Programming Standards (2010) should be used as a tool to understand the elements of a differentiated curriculum for the gifted learner. For university personnel, it would be helpful to review the gifted education teacher preparation standards (NAGC & CEC, 2006) to see the extent to which there is alignment to the new CCSS-ELA.

Below is a sampling of resources that might be considered in implementing the CCSS-ELA with gifted students.

English Language Arts Associations

International Reading Association (IRA) provides a website with a section dedicated to Common Core State Standards and links to readings about Common Core, reading, and literacy from the association's books and journals. Lesson plans, reading lists developed by children and teachers, position papers, and other resources about developing, assessing, and researching reading and literacy are provided available from http://www.reading.org/.

The National Council of Teachers of English (NCTE) provides combined NCTE/IRA Standards for the English Language Arts, supplementing state and national ELA standards. Links to lesson plans; readings for elementary, middle, and high school students; policy briefs; and resources specific to Common Core State Standards may be accessed from http://www.ncte.org/.

Assessment

Assessments for measuring the progress of gifted and talented students may be found in the *NAGC Pre-K–Grade 12 Gifted Education Programming Standards: A Guide to Planning and Implementing High-Quality Services* (Johnsen, 2012). Sulak and Johnsen (2012) described informal assessments that might be available without charge and used informally in assessing student outcomes in creativity, critical thinking, curriculum, interests, learning and motivation, and social–emotional areas. They also have identified specific product and performance assessments and other assessments that might be useful in program planning and evaluation. Although many of the assessments do not provide technical information, 23 of them do provide either reliability or validity information.

The Partnership for Assessment of Readiness for College and Careers (PARCC) is a 22-state consortium that has been formed to develop a common assessment system to measure the CCSS-ELA. To learn more about their work and the progress of their assessment development, visit http://www.parcconline.org.

Smarter Balanced Assessment Consortium is a state-led consortium working to develop assessments that are aligned to the CCSS-ELA. The web-based resources include the alignment of the CCSS-ELA to International Baccalaureate and the Texas

College Career Readiness Standards. To learn more about the consortium, alignments with other standards, and their progress on developing assessments for the standards, visit http://www. smarterbalanced.org.

Information regarding standardized achievement tests may be found in *Identifying Gifted Students: A Practical Guide* (Johnsen, 2011). In their chapter, "Technical Information Regarding Assessment," Robins and Jolly (2011) provided a list of 28 instruments that are frequently used in the identification of gifted students and their technical qualities. Because many of these assessments are also used to identify students who are above grade level in specific academic areas, they would be appropriate for measuring a gifted student's academic progress.

The importance of appropriate assessment of gifted students in order to show growth is highlighted in an NAGC service publication, *Alternative Assessments With Gifted Students* (VanTassel-Baska, 2008a). Separate chapters by noted authorities in gifted education focus on assessment issues related to both identification and learning. Inclusion of assessment models for use by schools in building program credibility through growth models is discussed. The book includes chapters on performance-based assessments, off-level assessment, products, and portfolios as more authentic ways to assess gifted student learning.

Curriculum and Instructional Strategies

The American Association of School Libraries (AASL) offers a lesson plan database that is searchable by grade, standards indicator, content topic, and keyword. Lessons are vetted by members of the AASL according to a rubric and checklist provided on the site. All lesson plans are aligned with a Common Core State Standard crosswalk developed by the organization. To access this database, visit http://aasl.jesandco.org.

Readwritethink.org is a website featuring classroom resources (i.e., lesson plans, student interactives, mobile apps) that is searchable by grade level, resource type, learning objective, and theme. Lessons are linked to Common Core State Standards and current state language arts standards. To read more, visit http://www.readwritethink.org.

EDSITEment: The Best of the Humanities on the Web is a site supported by the National Endowment for the Humanities. The site provides lesson plans in multiple content areas including language arts, and may be sorted by grade level or subtopic (including Common Core; AP literature; fables, fairytales, and folklore; and origin of literature). This tool can assist educators in locating CCSS-ELA-appropriate materials at various grade levels and provide above-level readings when searching by advanced grade level. Visit http://edsitement.neh.gov/lesson-plans.

Carnegie Mellon Institute for Talented Elementary and Secondary Students (C-MITES) offers resources/links to curriculum in mathematics, science, technology, engineering, language arts, and social studies. For more information, visit http://www.cmu.edu/cmites/.

The Center for Gifted Education at the College of William & Mary has designed curricular units in the areas of mathematics, language arts, science, and social studies that are based on the three dimensions of the Integrated Curriculum Model: advanced content, higher level processes and products, and interdisciplinary concepts, issues, and themes. The materials emphasize a sophistication of ideas, opportunities for extensions, the use of higher order thinking skills, and opportunities for student exploration based on interest. Specific teaching strategies are also described on the website including literature webs, the hamburger model for persuasive writing, vocabulary webs, the use of Paul's Elements of Reasoning, analyzing primary sources, and a research model for students. For more information about the units, visit the Center for Gifted Education at http://education. wm.edu/centers/cfge/curriculum/index.php.

The websites from the developers of the state assessments aligned with the CCSS provide news about tools that are being developed to support the Standards' implementation. For more information, visit http://www.smarterbalanced.org and http://www.parcconline.org.

The Davidson Institute for Talent Development offers links to resources in mathematics, language arts, science, social studies, arts and culture, and related domains. It also provides links to information about educational options, such as ability grouping, acceleration, enrichment programs, competitions, and other services. To explore these resources, visit http://www.davidson gifted.org/db/browse_by_topic_resources.aspx.

The Georgia Department of Education Common Core Standards website includes a searchable database of lesson plans aligned with the Common Core State Standards, video resources for professional development, and rubrics for text selection. The site may be accessed from https://www.georgiastandards.org/Pages/default.aspx.

The Illinois State Board of Education provides educator resources, which include progressions in mathematics, lesson examples, and links to other resources. To access these resources, visit http://www.isbe.net/common_core/htmls/resources.htm.

The Maine Department of Education provides resources for implementing the CCSS-ELA, which include performance tasks and examples of student writing. For implementing the CCSS for mathematics, they have developed three modules that provide an overview, alignment with other standards, and professional development modules. To access these resources, visit http://www.maine.gov/education/lres/commoncore/index.html.

The Neag Center for Gifted Education and Talent Development offers online resources that describe research studies and defensible practices in the field of gifted and talented education. Some of the studies address curriculum at the high school level, the explicit teaching of thinking skills, cluster grouping, algebraic understanding, reading with young children, differentiated performance assessments, and content-based curriculum. To access the studies, visit http://www.gifted.uconn.edu/nrcgt/nrconlin.html.

The Teaching Channel provides a video featuring one teacher's use of Socratic seminars in a high school classroom. Rationale for strategy, explanation of approach, benefits of implementation, and snippets of student conversation within and about Socratic Seminars are provided. Alignment with Common Core State Standards is provided beside the video. View *Socratic Seminar: Supporting Claims and Counterclaims* at https://www.teachingchannel.org/videos/using-socratic-seminars-in-classroom.

The Great Books Foundation is a nonprofit educational organization dedicated to the promotion of reading through the process of shared inquiry. The Great Books Foundation offers training in facilitating shared inquiry learning, textual analysis, and critical thinking skills in K–12 students. Materials include selections from classic texts. Information about training, grade-level materials, and free discussion guides to novels, poetry, drama, and philosophy are provided at http://www.greatbooks.org/programs-for-all-ages/junior.html.

Text Selection

The following resources are useful tools in guiding text selection and instructional approach appropriate to development, concept, theme, and genre.

Baskin, B. H., & Harris, K. H. (1980). *Books for the gifted child.* New York, NY: Bowker.

Baskin, B. H., Hauser, P., Harris, K. H., & Nelson, G. A. (1988). *Books for the gifted child* (Vol. 2). New York, NY: Bowker.

Halsted, J. W. (2009). *Some of my best friends are books: Guiding gifted readers from preschool to high school* (3rd ed.). Tuscon, AZ: Great Potential Press.

Thompson, M. C. (1994). *Classics in the classroom.* Unionville, NY: Royal Fireworks.

Thompson, M. C. (1994). *Word within the word: An exploration of the interior language for academically motivated secondary students* (Vol. 1). Unionville, NY: Royal Fireworks.

Thompson, M. C. (1995). *The magic lens*. Unionville, NY: Royal Fireworks.

Wisconsin Association for Talented and Gifted. (2011). *Giftedness and literacy: Resources from Dr. Penny Kolloff.* Retrieved from http://www.watg.org/giftedness-and-literacy.html

Language Arts Pathways for Advanced Learners

Although the NAGC Programming Standards (2010) note that students must receive advanced curriculum content and social-emotional support, curriculum can be a tool to significantly advance student thinking. The study of language arts can lead to a wide variety of vocational and nonvocational options from the practical career options of law, business, and politics to the more expressive careers of novelists, lyricists, and poets. It is critically important that advanced students receive appropriate activities at different levels of schooling that will expose them to a broader world, provoke interest, define their passions, and develop their abilities. Sometimes called "trajectories" in terms of determining which activities should occur at which levels of schooling, the language arts are so broad and such an integral component of so many possible careers and interest areas, the term "pathways" has been used here to help schools and districts in their planning processes.

The concept of a pathway from innate ability to developed talent is derived from the Gagné (2000) model of talent development that posits starting with abilities in different domains that become converted into developed talents in various fields through time, learning, and specific practice routines. The interaction between personal characteristics and external environmental factors can fashion a creative, productive professional life if the outside events are provided to students who express passion and interest in the language arts.

It may be important to lay out certain assumptions about our thinking in this regard:

- Talent development is a larger process than what happens during K–12 and is certainly bigger than what happens in school. Many of the experiences that matter for these students, based on the literature that informs our understanding of talented adults, occur outside of school and in more informal contexts that allow for the hours of practice necessary to convert skills to talents.
- The factors that influence the talent development process must merge in important ways: The individual must be willing to devote time and energy to a particular type of endeavor over multiple years and receive the instruction and support in that area that will fuel performance.
- The levels of talent that are reached may be affected by many variables, which include initial abilities, hours of deliberate practice, and the role of life occurrences that may inhibit as well as propel the person forward in the process. Thus, advanced learners may or may not fulfill their talent potential.

These pathways of certain skills should serve as guides and activity foci for gifted programs that emphasize development in the language arts. The CCSS-ELA support these pathways of skills, which include the development of:

- proficiency in the content standards,
- critical thinking,
- creative thinking,
- problem solving,
- metacognition,
- identity development, and
- collaboration.

Skill Pathways

Proficiency in the content areas. Through the use of the argumentative essays required in the CCSS-ELA, students can provide reasoning and support for their own thinking in the content area. In order to deepen content understanding, students must reason within them. First, the use of critical reading behaviors allows students to grow and expand within the content areas. Although the CCSS-ELA have been criticized for their heavy emphasis on nonfiction reading, the critical reading behaviors of analysis and integration of concepts cut across all content areas. By being close, fluent, and highly proficient readers, advanced students can make better sense of information.

Secondly, in order to realize their potential, gifted and advanced students must be able to communicate expressively with others within a given content area. The increased fluency in writing that is developed through the CCSS-ELA and the ensuing differentiation allows students to more appropriately target their message. Through the increasing mastery of form and function of writing with purpose and audience, advanced students can achieve communication in a wide variety of content areas. Coupled with presentation skills of oral and visual media, advanced students can better achieve the purpose of their communication.

Lastly, the language arts help advanced students organize and present their information in a coherent manner. Care should be taken that assessments and products emphasize the critical thinking that is necessary to produce coherency when communicating with others.

Critical thinking. The CCSS-ELA and the differentiated tasks encourage students to develop strong forms of communication. Elder and Paul (2007) noted that concepts and ideas are used to "interpret data, facts, and experiences in order to answer questions, solve problems, and resolve issues" (p. 3). The most common form of writing emphasized is persuasive writing because it is an excellent tool to develop analysis. The analysis needed to understand a point of view that may be different from one's own and the ability to match the communication to that audience for a particular purpose is a critical skill. This skill allows an advanced student to recognize the implicit and explicit assumptions that are in place for various audiences and to target communication to suit the purpose. These communication skills can provide clarity of purpose and a deeper understanding of the content. By recognizing the inferences that are implicit in the data to be selected and communicated, an advanced student moves from being the receiver of data to being the creator and synthesizer of data. The final step of this critical-thinking process is the determination of possible implications and consequences of a particular course of action. The communication that results from understanding the use and purpose of argument and persuasion is a skill necessary in the process of becoming a leader.

Creative thinking. Critical and creative thinking are both necessary elements to drive progress. Creative thinking allows advanced students to synthesize new ideas through determining abstract understandings. By understanding commonalities and differences, advanced students can generate and extract generalizations that determine relationships. Creativity implies sustained, concentrated attention to small details that form a larger whole. As Steve Jobs (1995) said, "Creativity is just connecting things" (para. 124) Understanding what is being connected implies a deeper understanding of the details. Through this exploration of relationships between and within different content areas, media, and concepts, advanced students can develop innovative approaches to problems.

Problem solving. The key element of problem solving, too often overlooked in traditional multiple-choice style teaching and learning, is problem finding and identification. This involves a set of decision-making processes that are both implicit and explicit as students define the boundaries of their "problem." The process of language arts is a process of problem finding, in which advanced students must determine the purpose and issue that language is addressing. Gifted students can explore the inherent problems in their field of choice, including that of communication and expressive arts, and the range of possible solutions. As Eliot Eisner (2004) said, "The arts teach children that in complex forms of problem solving purposes are seldom fixed, but change with circumstance and opportunity" (p. 82). By using words and language as the media, advanced students can explore the range of possible solutions through communication. Implied in this process is the need for research, as advanced students must explore what others have determined to be problems and their resultant solutions. This need for research grounds the language arts in the "real world," whether that real world be one that is imagination-based, or societally defined. Whether the "problem" is a poetical expression, or capturing the drama of a moment, or communicating to change minds, the language arts possess a wide range of expression. And by addressing the use of language arts as a means of problem finding and solving, advanced students can explore the limits of their chosen medium, determining what can be generalized to new situations and what cannot be. Finally, the use of language arts in a problem-solving aspect allows advanced students to explore the ethical and moral implications of choices.

Metacognitive thinking. Choices are determined when students can explicitly make determinations about what is possible. That process of making the implicit explicit directly impacts the development of metacognition. Involved in this process is the need to reflect and ponder on available choices and to reflect not just on the product, but on the process as well. From an understanding of how the product can be created, an understanding of the process can emerge. The student can then be more efficient in his planning of future products.

Identity development. Perhaps the most powerful element of the need to differentiate the curriculum in language arts is the ability of language arts to promote self-awareness and self-understanding. Words and their usage are tools through which advanced students share themselves, and consequently, determine who they are. By using words, ideas and understandings are shaped and created. Deepening their own personal identity allows students to deepen their own contributions.

Collaboration. Language arts provide a foundation for leadership in any content area because the use of language allows communication that provides the opportunity for collaboration between individuals. By problem solving with others, leadership opportunities emerge for myriad career paths.

Through differentiation and the provision of specific skills within language arts, advanced children have the opportunity to continue to learn and develop and grow, providing themselves with a sense of mission and purpose and our country with our future leaders.

Implications for Schools

It is suggested that schools and districts provide a plan for talent development by completing a grid (such as the one in Figure 2) that will allow them to create opportunities within their own context. Opportunities to work on the goals described in Figure 2 can provide students with significant experiences that can help lead them into a productive career and life that involves language arts.

When designing these activities, there are several factors to consider. Many of them are contextual in nature: availability of resources, capacity, particular passion areas of the students, etc. But there is a significant need to combine the advanced intellect of the child with the developmental aspects of the child's social and emotional needs.

Stages of Development

Early years. Some of these interventions crucial at early stages of development include finding a peer group of students with similar interests and abilities who can work together. Grouping of gifted learners early is a spur to their developing abilities and interests in a verbal area. This is especially important for verbal learners, as research suggests that their growth and development is dependent on the verbal transaction process of

Goals	K–2 Activities	3–5 Activities	6–8 Activities	9–12 Activities
Proficiency				
Critical Thinking				
Creative Thinking				
Problem Solving				
Identity Development				
Metacognitive				
Collaboration				

Figure 2. Talent development grid.

trying out ideas as they are formulated (VanTassel-Baska, Zuo, Avery, & Little, 2002). Also critical at this early stage is providing rich experiences in all of the verbal arts stimulus areas, including reading, writing, viewing, drawing, and speaking. After a time, advanced learners may gravitate more to one area of the verbal arts than others by showing a clear preference for speaking, writing, or reading. Because we know that reading feeds the souls of writers, this preference may not signal a career path but merely an early preparatory predisposition.

Middle years. At the next level of development, advanced learners become more serious about their preferences and how they use time in pursuit of their talent. Gifted and advanced students may enter writing or forensic competitions to establish benchmarks that delineate their current progress and show how much advancement is needed to improve significantly at the process. Tutors or mentors who can provide assistance in the acquisition of skills at this stage of development can be valuable. In addition, it may be helpful to identify writers to emulate and serve as role models for spurring higher level development of a particular form. Other instruction and supports for growing interest at this stage include extracurricular camps and online programs in the summer or on Saturdays. Some students may begin to take world languages to hone skills and expand their vision and understanding of other cultures. In turn, this knowledge aids in self-understanding and cultivates the empathy needed to develop meaningful relationships with others. Reflection on one's potential talent fields and a clear assessment of one's own strengths and weaknesses in the talent areas provide another basis for judgment about how interested an advanced learner may remain in a worthwhile domain.

Adolescence. By adolescence, the development of talent becomes more refined as advanced learners have opportunities to test out their skills in the adult world of work through apprenticeships and internships that provide glimpses of a future life that they may wish to experience. Their knowledge and skill bank is also growing through advanced in-school opportunities like

Advanced Placement (AP) or International Baccalaureate (IB) English, History, or World Languages courses. Experiences at colleges and universities in coursework, in college and career planning, and in school-based advanced programs offer additional support during these years as the talent area emerges at a higher level, fueled also by performance and portfolio opportunities to showcase the actual work produced by the advanced learner at this stage. Competitions at the national and international levels become important to motivate the learner to higher levels of excellence in the selected area. Self-assessment becomes more integral to the advanced learner's decision making about colleges and programs of study that may be the optimal match for the evolving talent.

The Role of Schools in Talent Development

So what is the role of schools in this process? Can they become important brokers and facilitators of talent development, or do they become barriers to it by imposing cumbersome rules and regulations that block advanced learners from their upward trajectory of progress in a talent area? Hopefully, schools can begin to see how they can support the talent development process by becoming more flexible in how students are educated, when and where they are educated, and the levels of attainment that may be relevant given the students' advanced capacity and developed skills. For schools, the challenge is to step aside and find the optimal match for these students at a given point in time (Bloom, 1985). It is often not a desired role, as it requires humility in the face of a student who cannot be well served by the existing system, creativity in finding the right resources that will help, and the follow-through to ensure that the intervention works for this advanced learner at a particular point in time. Counselors, teachers, and administrators all play important roles in this process of designing appropriate alternative intervention plans for advancing talent in specific learners, both individually and collectively.

Schools have an obligation not to make advanced learners "prisoners of time," and to ensure that their learning time is used efficiently and effectively as they traverse the grades (National Education Commission on Time and Learning, 1994). In suburban districts, that may mean being allowed to advance to the next level of coursework. In rural districts, it may mean having access to online coursework such as AP courses, which can be taken asynchronously. In specialized schools for the gifted, such as the New Orleans Center for Creative Arts, it may mean having an artist mentor working in a tutorial for portfolio development in lieu of classes one day a week. All of these options are appropriate for advanced learners, depending on the possibilities and constraints of the context.

Schools also have a special obligation to students from poverty to help them develop their talents. Unlike more affluent youngsters, these students lack the means of family support and resources that provide lessons, tutors, and extracurricular experiences through summer and academic year special programs (VanTassel-Baska, 2010). It is the schools themselves that must find creative ways to provide experiences to spawn the interest, the motivation, and the skill development necessary to make these students competitive in their desired future careers. A focus on a print-rich environment, vocabulary development, and discussion opportunities linked to writing all provide needed enrichment for such students. Special programs and services geared to these students must also be planned and executed so that talent is not denied based on means.

Implications for Professional Learning When Implementing the CCSS-ELA

Professional learning is essential for all educators who ideally are engaged in learning communities to identify specific knowledge and skills needed to serve different groups of learners (Learning Forward, 2011). Teachers and content specialists should collaborate in learning communities to identify specific knowledge and skills needed to serve different groups of learners. As schools and school districts adopt and begin using the CCSS-ELA, all educators should be involved in ongoing learning to address the needs of gifted and high-potential students. Specifically, all educators need a repertoire of research-supported strategies to deliberately adapt and modify curriculum, instruction, and assessment within the framework of the CCSS-ELA, based on the needs of gifted and talented students as well as those with high potential.

Although the CCSS-ELA provide the framework for the learning experiences for all students, gifted educators need focused training that is content-specific for differentiating the standards (VanTassel-Baska, 2008b; VanTassel-Baska et al., 2008). Systematic professional development will support all educators to adapt, modify, or replace the CCSS-ELA based on the needs of the learner. To differentiate effectively for gifted and high-potential learners, all educators need to develop expertise at *designing learning experiences and assessments that are conceptually advanced, challenging, and complex.* In the English language arts area, three types of training are recommended for teachers:

- Training that is focused on building content expertise: How do I become more proficient in literature, writing, and language in order to work effectively with gifted and advanced students?
- Training that is focused on differentiating language arts pedagogy: How do I learn to teach literature, writing, and language to the gifted? What pedagogical tools will help me?
- Training that is focused on implementing research-based differentiated language arts programs: How do I implement Junior Great Books, the William & Mary language arts units, and/or the *Jacob's Ladder Reading Comprehension Program* into my classroom?

Professional development for implementing the CCSS–ELA for gifted and high-ability learners should focus on evidence-based differentiation practices as they relate to specific core content. The training should demonstrate how to apply acceleration strategies; how to add depth and complexity elements such as critical thinking, creative thinking, problem solving, and inquiry; and how to develop and encourage creativity, all within the CCSS-ELA. In addition to the curriculum adaptation and modification, the professional development experiences should also demonstrate content-specific ways to design and implement differentiated product-based assessments as well as pre- and postassessments appropriate for advanced students. However, gifted educators are in no way expected to be experts in all content areas; therefore, it is imperative to develop collaborative relationships with skilled content specialists to provide knowledgeable advice, content-specific peer coaching services and pedagogical knowledge while implementing the CCSS-ELA.

Examples of Professional Learning Models for Implementing the CCSS-ELA

Educators should take an active role in designing learning options to facilitate their learning and improvement of student results (Learning Forward, 2011). Active learning may include of the following elements:

- discussion and dialogue,
- coaching and modeling,
- demonstration and reflection,
- inquiry and problem solving, and
- tiered model of professional learning experiences.

Collaboration With General and Special Education

It cannot be emphasized enough that gifted education professionals must collaborate with other educational partners and not "go it alone" in the process of implementing the CCSS-ELA on behalf of advanced learners and their talent development process. Gifted educators' roles include direct service and advocacy for the gifted child, including academic, social, and emotional development. As part of their training, gifted educators have extensive knowledge of strategy instruction, which allows for a deep understanding of pedagogy. There are numerous partners with whom it is important to collaborate, depending on the specific needs and abilities of the child. In the language arts area, collaborating with librarians and media personnel is especially helpful in the selection of appropriate reading materials and in the implementation of discussions about text. Working with local writers also provides students with the real–world connection to the skills they are learning and an opportunity to see how writers practice their craft. Finally, in the language arts area, collaboration with other arts areas such as theater companies, curators at museums, and civic orchestras provides students the opportunity to see connections to how literature is only one art form that provides a window to our understanding of the world.

Role of Administrators

Within their roles as gatekeepers and managers of the entire educational process, administrators must be included in discussions of systemic talent development. Rather than making talent development a highly individualistic, ad hoc process, administrators play a key role in systematizing an educational program that can provide progression within the disciplines for talented students. For school principals and curriculum directors, this role is essential to be assumed. Full participation in and sanction of differentiation of the CCSS-ELA for gifted learners is the first step in making such adaptations a reality. Because teachers need to collaborate across grade levels to make the adaptations easily, administrators must organize vertical planning teams and provide resources in the form of time and support for such efforts. Principals also need to monitor for implementation of these adaptations once they have been developed.

Conclusion

This second book in adapting the Common Core English Language Arts standards for advanced learners provides classroom teachers and administrators examples and strategies to implement the new CCSS-ELA at various stages of development across the years in K–12 schools. Toward this goal, this text clarifies what advanced opportunities may look like for such learners from primary through secondary grade levels. Often, "typical" examples were drawn directly from state websites for curriculum suggestions and were then differentiated. To provide learners challenging learning experiences, this book provides examples of differentiated learning through advanced readings, creative thinking and production, connections to other ELA standards, including writing and speaking/listening, and, when relevant, connections to interdisciplinary standards. Additionally, the examples provided in this text incorporate choices for students, research opportunities, and higher level questions for individual, small-group, and whole-class discussion. To illustrate the differentiation by task demand, learning experiences for general education students and advanced learners are paired by standard. Suggested readings, activities, and assessments are indicated to provide educators with resources that are aligned and are appropriate to the standard, grade level, and level of difficulty appropriate to the respective learner. An assessment section delineates issues in addressing the needs of the gifted learner through differentiated assessments, tailored to the archetypal activities designed. Rubrics are suggested for use and as models for further development by teachers. Additionally, the authors provide scope and sequence outlines for the reading literature and reading informational text standards to illustrate between-grade progression of the standards and to inform educators of directional choices for guiding advanced learners in their development beyond the grade-level standards as needed. The authors also suggest a scope and sequence of language arts work for the gifted that is consonant with the NAGC curriculum standards for school-based programs.

In sum, this text provides guidance for educators in developing differentiated learning experiences using the CCSS-ELA and for continued refinement of on-level and above-level learning experiences to challenge advanced learners. Using this book as a guide, teachers can likewise develop differentiated learning experiences tied to the remaining CCSS-ELA with key principles of differentiation in mind.

References

Allen, A. (2012). *Creating the code: Navajo code talkers declassified.* Retrieved from http://47607609.nhd.weebly.com/index.html

Anti-Defamation League. (2012). *The Ten Commandments in the public square.* Retrieved from http://www.adl.org/assets/pdf/civil-rights/religiousfreedom/religiousfreeres/TenCommands-docx.pdf

Barenaked Ladies. (2013). The Big Bang Theory theme. From *Hits from yesterday and the day before.* Los Angeles, CA: Warner Bros. Music.

Bartusik, M. (2010). *The day we found the universe.* New York, NY: Vintage.

Bloom, B. S. (Ed.). (1985). *Developing talent in young people.* New York, NY: Ballantine.

Bruchac, J. (2006). *Code talkers: A novel about the Navajo Marines of World War II.* Tallahassee, FL: Speak.

Bulfinch, T. (2008). *Bulfinch's mythology.* New York, NY: Barnes & Noble Classics.

Camus, A. (2005). *Myth of Sisyphus.* New York, NY: Penguin. (Original work published in 1942)

Carson, M. K. (2008). *Exploring the solar system: A history with 22 activities*. Chicago, IL: Chicago Review Press.

Center for Gifted Education. (n.d.). *Language arts curriculum*. Retrieved from http://education.wm.edu/centers/cfge/curriculum/languagearts/index.php

Corera, G. (2012). *WWII pigeon message stumps GCHQ decoders*. BBC News. Retrieved from http://www.bbc.co.uk/news/uk-20456782

Council of Chief State School Officers. (2011). *InTASC model core teaching standards: A resource for state dialogue*. Retrieved from http://www.ccsso.org/resources/programs/interstate_teacher_assessment_consortium_%28intasc%29.html

Daily, D. (2007). *The classic treasury of Aesop's fables*. Philadelphia, PA: Running Press.

de Maupassant, G. (1909). Ugly. In *The Works of Guy de Maupassant* (Vol. I, pp. 376–379). Retrieved from http://www.gutenberg.org/zipcat.php/21327/21327-h/21327-h.htm#Page_376

Descartes, R. (1993). *Meditations on first philosophy: In which the existence of God and the distinction of the soul from the body are demonstrated*. Cambridge, MA: Hackett. (Original work published in 1641)

Douglass, F. (2005). *A narrative of the life of Frederick Douglass*. New York, NY: Dover. (Original work published in 1845)

Eisner, E. (2004). *Arts and the education of the mind*. New Haven, CT: Yale University Press.

Elder, L. & Paul, R. (2007). *Thinker's guide to analytic thinking*. Sonoma, CA: Center for Critical Thinking.

Evans, B., & Harland, D. M. (2008). *NASA's Voyager missions: Exploring the outer solar system and beyond*. New York, NY: Springer.

Fletcher, L. (2012). I am the moon. In J.VanTassel-Baska & T. Stambaugh (Eds.), *Jacob's ladder student poetry workbook* (pp. 8). Waco, TX: Prufrock Press.

Franklin, B. (1996). *The autobiography of Benjamin Franklin*. New York, NY: Dover. (Original work published in 1791)

Frost, R. (2009). The road not taken. In R. Frost (Author) *Mountain interval* (p. 9). Gloucester, UK: Dodo Press. (Original work published 1916)

Gagné, F. (2000). Understanding the complex choreography of talent development through DMGT-based analysis. In K. A. Heller, F. J. Mönks, R. J. Sternberg, & R. Subotnik (Eds.), *International handbook for research on giftedness and talent* (2nd ed., pp. 67–79). Oxford, UK: Pergamon.

Georgia Department ot Education. (2013). English language arts education forum. Retrieved from http://georgiaelaccgpsk-5. wikispaces.com

Ghandi, M. K. (2008). *Autobiography: The story of my experiments with truth.* Thousand Oaks, CA: BN. (Original work published in 1927)

Great Books Foundation. (n.d.a). *Junior great books.* Retrieved from http://www.greatbooks.org/programs–for–all–ages/ junior/jgbseries/

Great Books Foundation. (n.d.b). Middle and high school critical thinking rubric. In *The Great Books Foundation middle and high school assessment tools* (pp. 7). Retrieved from http:// www.greatbooks.org/fileadmin/pdf/JGB_7-9_IGB_1-3.pdf

Great Books Foundation. (n.d.c). Middle and high school writing rubric. In *The Great Books Foundation middle and high dchool sssessment tools* (p. 12–13). Retrieved from http://www.great-books.org/fileadmin/pdf/JGB_7-9_IGB_1-3.pdf

Hanna, J., & Holub, J. (2006). *The man who named the clouds.* New York, NY: Albert Whitman.

Hawthorne, N. (1994). *The Scarlet Letter.* Mineola, NY: Dover. (Original work published 1850)

Henry, O. (2008). *The gift of the magi.* Somerville, MA: Candlewick Press. (Original work published 1906)

History Channel. (2013a). *The Statue of Liberty.* Retrieved from http://www.history.com/topics/statue-of-liberty/vid-eos#the-statue-of-liberty

History Channel. (2013b). *Statue of Liberty unknown*. Retrieved from http://www.history.com/topics/statue-of-liberty/videos#statue-of-liberty-unknown

Homer. (1998). *The iliad*. New York, NY: Penguin. (Original work written *ca.* 1260 BC)

Indiana Department of Public Instruction. (2013). *Indiana High Ability Project (HAP) in English Language Arts (ELA)*. Indianapolis: Author.

Jackson, S. (2005). *The lottery and other stories* (2nd ed.). New York, NY: Farrar, Strauss and Giroux. (Original work published in 1949)

Jefferson, T. (1786). T*he Virginia act for establilshing religious freedom*. Retrieved from http://www.religiousfreedom.lib.virginia.edu/sacred/vaact.html

Jobs, S. (1995, April). The next insanely great thing. *Wired*. Retrieved from http://www.wired.com/wired/archive/4.02/jobs_pr.html

Johnsen, S. K. (Ed.). (2011). *Identifying gifted students: A practical guide* (2nd ed.). Waco, TX: Prufrock Press.

Johnsen, S. K. (Ed.). (2012). *NAGC Pre-K–Grade 12 gifted education programming standards: A guide to planning and implementing high-quality services*. Waco, TX: Prufrock Press.

Johnsen, S. K., & Sheffield, L. J. (Eds.). (2013). *Using the common core state standards for mathematics with gifted and advanced learners*. Waco, TX: Prufrock Press.

Juster, N. (1988). *The phantom tollbooth*. New York, NY: Yearling, Bullseye Books. (Original work published in 1961)

Kansas Department of Education. (n.d.). *Grade 5 narrative writing rubric*. Retrieved from http://www.ksde.org/LinkClick.aspx?fileticket=ydnSqQjPfxA%3D&tabid=145&mid=4738

Kaplan, R. (2000). *The nothing that is: A natural history of zero*. New York, NY: Oxford University Press.

King, M. L., Jr. (1990). *I have a dream/Letter from a Birmingham jail*. Logan, IA: Perfection Learning. (Original works written in 1963)

Kipling, R. (2013). *If.* Retrieved from http://www.kipling.org. uk/poems_if.htm (Original work published in 1910)

Landis, B. (2012). *Carlisle Indian industrial school.* Retrieved from http://home.epix.net?˜landis/

Lawrence, D. H. (2007). *The rocking horse winner.* Logan, IA: Perfection Learning. (Original work published in 1926)

Lazarus, E. (1883). *The new colossus.* Retrieved from http://xroads. virginia.edu/˜cap/liberty/lazaruspoem.html

Learning Forward. (2011). *Standards for professional learning: Learning communities.* Retrieved from http://www.learning-forward.org/standards/learningcommunities/index.cfm

Linder, D. (2001). *The trial of Susan B. Anthony for illegal voting.* Retrieved from http://law2umkc.edu/faculty/projects/ftrials/ anthony/sbahome.html

Lindsey, V. (1919). The moon's the north wind's cooky. In V. Lindsey, *The Congo and other poems* (p.X). Retrieved from http://xroads.virginia.edu/˜hyper/Lindsay/lindsay.html-l#themoons

Locker, T. (2003). *Cloud dance.* New York, NY: Houghton Mifflin.

Malory, T. (1970). *Le morte d'Arthur.* New York, NY: Penguin. (Original work published in 1485)

Measured Progress/ETS Collaborative. (2012). *Smarter balanced English language arts item and task specifications.* Retrieved from http://www.smarterbalanced.org

Meyers, W. D. (2001). *Bad boy: A memoir.* New York, NY: HarperCollins.

Miller, R., & Wilson, K. (1997). *Making and enjoying telescopes.* New York, NY: Sterling.

Moon, T., Brighton, C. M., Callahan, C. M., & Robinson, A. (2005). Development of authentic assessments for middle school classrooms. *Journal of Secondary Gifted Education, 16,* 119–133.

Murphy, J. (2000). *Blizzard.* New York, NY: Scholastic.

NASA. (2013). *Mars laboratory images.* Retrieved from http:// www.nasa.gov/mission_pages/msl/images/index.html

National Archives. (2013a). *Memorandum regarding the enlistment of Navajo Indians.* Retrieved from http://www.archives.gov/education/lessons/code-talkers

National Archives. (2013b). *Woman suffrage in Washington, District of Columbia.* Retrieved from http://docsteach.org/documents/533773/detail

National Association for Gifted Children. (2010). *Pre-K–grade 12 gifted programming standards.* Retrieved from http://www.nagc.org/ProgrammingStandards.aspx

National Association for Gifted Children, & Council for Exceptional Children. (2006). *NAGC-CEC teacher knowledge and skills for gifted and talented education.* Retrieved from http://www.nagc.org/NCATEStandards.aspx

National Assessment Governing Board. (2008). *Reading framework for the 2009 National Assessment of Educational Progress.* Retrieved from http://www.nagb.org/publications/frameworks/reading09.pdf

National Assessment Governing Board. (2010). *Writing framework for the 2011 National Assessment of Educational Progress.* Retrieved from http://www.nagb.org/publications/frameworks/writing-2011.pdf

National Education Commission on Time and Learning. (1994). *Prisoners of time.* Retrieved from http://www2.ed.gov/pubs/PrisonersOfTime/index.html

National Governors Association Center for Best Practices, & Council of Chief State School Officers. (2010). *Common core state standards in English language arts.* Retrieved from http://www.corestandards.org/the-standards

National Park Service. (2013). *Statue of Liberty.* Retrieved from http://www.nps.gov/featurecontent/stli/eTour.htm

National Weather Service. (2002). *A guide to developing a severe weather emergency plan for schools.* Retrieved from http://www.erh.noaa.gov/er/lwx/swep

Newcomb, T. (2012, February 20). A brief history of (what you think is) Presidents' Day: The first thing to know is it's not officially called Presidents' Day. *Time.* Retrieved from http://

newsfeed.time.com/2012/02/20/a-brief-history-of-what-you-think-is-presidents-day

Nez, C., & Avila, J. S. (2012). *Code talker: The first and only memoir by one of the original Navajo code talkers of WWII.* New York, NY: Berkeley Trade.

O'Brien, P. (2009). *You are the first kid on Mars.* New York, NY: Putnam Juvenile.

Partnership for 21st Century Skills Framework for 21st Century Learning. (n.d.). *Framework for 21st century learning.* Retrieved from http://www.p21.org/overview

Plato. (2000). *The republic.* New York, NY: Dover. (Original work published *ca.* 380 BC)

Poe, E. A. (2013). *Edgar Allan Poe: Complete tales and poems.* Seattle, WA: Magnolia Books.

Poetry Out Loud. (2012). *Poetry out loud scoring rubric.* Retrieved from http://www.poetryoutloud.org/uploads/fl/af34c39739/scoring%20rubric.pdf

ReadWriteThink. (2004). *Persuasive writing scoring guide.* Retrieved from http://www.readwritethink.org/files/resources/lesson_images/lesson405/PersuasiveWritingScoringGuide.pdf

ReadWriteThink. (2010). *Oral presentation rubric.* Retrieved from http://www.readwritethink.org/files/resources/print-outs/30700_rubric.pdf

Robb, D. (2007). *Ox, house, stick: The history of our alphabet.* Watertown, MA: Charlesbridge.

Robins, J. H., & Jolly, J. L. (2011). Technical information regarding assessment. In S. K. Johnsen (Ed.), *Identifying gifted students: A practical guide* (2nd ed., pp. 75–188). Waco, TX: Prufrock Press.

Rorty, R. (1990). The priority of democracy to philosophy. In R. Rorty, *Objectivity, relativism, and truth: Philosophical papers, volume 1* (pp. 175–197). Cambridge, England: Cambridge University Press.

Ruckman, I. (2003). *Night of the twisters.* New York, NY: HarperCollins.

Sagan, C. (1978). *Murmurs of Earth: The Voyager interstellar record.* New York, NY: Ballantine.

Scott, E. (1998). *Close encounters: Exploring the universe with the Hubble Space Telescope.* Anaheim, CA: Disney Productions.

Seaver, B. (2012). *Hurricanes at the dinner table.* Washington, DC: National Geographic Society. Retrieved from http://newswatch.nationalgeographic.com/2012/11/01/hurricane-at-the-dinner-table

Shakespeare, W. (2003). *Julius Caesar.* New York, NY: Simon & Schuster. (Original work written *ca.* 1599)

Shakespeare, W. (2004). *Macbeth.* New York, NY: Simon & Schuster. (Original work written *ca.* 1606)

Singer, M. (2001). *On the same day in March: A tour of the world's weather.* New York, NY: Harper Festival.

Stambaugh, T. (2011). Aligning curriculum for the gifted with content standards and state assessments. In J. VanTassel-Baska & C. A. Little (Eds.), *Content-based curriculum for high-ability learners* (2nd ed., pp. 397–412). Waco, TX: Prufrock Press.

Steig, W. (1982). *Doctor De Soto.* New York, NY: Farrar, Straus, and Girroux.

Steig, W. (1987). *Sylvester and the magic pebble.* New York, NY: Simon & Schuster.

Stevenson, R. L. (1913). *Moon.* In R. L. Stevenson, *A child's garden of verses* (p. 35). Retrieved from http://etc.usf.edu/lit2go/59/a-childs-garden-of-verses-selected-poems/4728/the-moon/ (Original work published in 1855)

Sulak, T. N., & Johnsen, S. K. (2012). Assessments for measuring student outcomes. In S. K. Johnsen (Ed.), *NAGC Pre-K–Grade 12 gifted education programming standards: A guide to planning and implementing high-quality services* (pp. 283–306). Waco, TX: Prufrock Press.

Tarshis, L. (2011). *I survived Hurricane Katrina.* New York, NY: Scholastic.

Thoreau, H. D. (1998). *A week on the Concord and Merrimack Rivers.* New York, NY: Penguin. (Original work published in 1849)

Time for Kids. (2013). Presidents' Day dilemma. *Time for Kids.* Retrieved from http://www. timeforkids.com/news/presidentsdaydilemma/29951

Tomlinson, C. A. (1999). *The differentiated classroom: Responding to the needs of all learners.* Alexandria, VA: Association of Supervision and Curriculum Development.

VanTassel-Baska, J. (2003). *Curriculum planning and instructional design for gifted learners.* Denver, CO: Love.

VanTassel-Baska, J. (Ed.). (2008a). *Alternative assessments with gifted students.* Waco, TX: Prufrock Press.

VanTassel-Baska, J. (2008b). An effective, standards-based professional development model for gifted education. In M. Kitano, D. Montgomery, J. VanTassel-Baska, & S. Johnsen (Eds.), *Using the national gifted education standards for preK–12 professional development* (pp. 49–54). Thousand Oaks, CA: Corwin Press.

VanTassel-Baska, J. (Ed.). (2010). *Patterns and profiles of promising learners from poverty.* Waco, TX: Prufrock Press.

VanTassel-Baska, J. (Ed.). (2013). *Using the common core state standards for English language arts with gifted and advanced learners.* Waco, TX: Prufrock Press.

VanTassel-Baska, J., Feng, A., Brown, E., Bracken, B., Stambaugh, T., & French, H. (2008). A study of differentiated instructional change over three years. *Gifted Child Quarterly, 52,* 297–312.

VanTassel-Baska, J., & Stambaugh, T. (Eds.). (2008). *What works: 20 years of curriculum development and research for advanced learners.* Waco, TX: Prufrock Press.

VanTassel-Baska, J., Zuo, L., Avery, L., & Little, C. A. (2002). A curriculum study of gifted-student learning in the language arts. *Gifted Child Quarterly, 46,* 30–43.

Warner, G. (2010). *The boxcar children bookshelf.* Park Ridge, IL: Albert Whitman.

Wiesel, E. (2006). *Night.* New York, NY: Macmillan. (Original work published in 1955)

Williams, W. C. (1985). *Selected poems.* New York, NY: New Directions.

Winona State University. (n.d.). *Class debate rubric.* Retrieved from http://www.course1.winona.edu/shatfield/air/classde-bate.pdf

X, M. (2001). *The autobiography of Malcolm X.* New York, NY: Penguin. (Original work published in 1965)

Appendix A
Definitions of Key Terms

Acceleration is a broad term used to describe ways in which gifted student learning may occur at a faster, more appropriate rate throughout the years of schooling. It refers to content acceleration through compacting and reorganizing curriculum by unit or year, grade skipping, telescoping 2 years into one, dual enrollment in high school and college or university, as well as more personalized approaches, such as tutorials and mentorships that also would be sensitive to the advanced starting level of these learners for instruction. Both Advanced Placement (AP) and International Baccalaureate (IB) at the high school level represent programs of study already accelerated in content. AP courses also may be taken on a fast track schedule earlier as appropriate.

Appropriate pacing refers to the rate at which material is taught to advanced learners. Because they are capable of mastering new material more rapidly than typical learners, appropriate pacing would involve careful preassessment and streamlining techniques to ensure that advanced learners are not bored with the material and are being adequately challenged. Note that although students might advance quickly through some material, they should also be given time to delve more deeply into topics of interest at appropriate advanced levels of complexity and innovation.

Assessment is the way to determine the scope and degree of learning that has been internalized by the student. For purposes of gifted education, the assessments must be matched to differentiated outcomes, requiring the use of authentic approaches like performance-based and portfolio-based assessment demands. Some assessments are already constructed and available for use, exhibiting strong technical adequacy and employed in research studies while others may be teacher-developed, with opportunities to establish interrater reliability among teachers who may be using them in schools. Care should be taken to use assessments that do not restrict the level of proficiency that students can demonstrate, such as above-grade-level assessments that allow for innovative and more complex responses.

Characteristics and needs of gifted learners is the basis for differentiating any curriculum area. In English language arts, verbally talented students learn to read early, talk in complex sentences, write coherent text, and become sensitive to language at an earlier stage of development than typical learners do. Because of this advanced readiness to engage with their world, their curriculum diet may be accelerated and should be advanced, rich in experiences for increasing complexity and depth, and open-ended to allow for creative manipulation of ideas and concepts.

Complexity refers to a feature of differentiation that provides advanced learners more variables to study, asks them to use multiple resources to solve a problem, or requires them to use multiple higher order skills simultaneously. The degree of complexity may depend on the developmental level of the learner, the nature of the learning task, and the readiness to take on the level of challenge required.

Creativity and innovation are used to suggest that activities used with the gifted employ opportunities for more open-ended project work that mirrors real-world professional work in solving problems in the disciplines. The terms also suggest that advanced learners will be able to internalize the skills and habits of mind associated with being a creator or innovator in a chosen field of endeavor. Thus, creative thinking and problem-solving skills would be emphasized.

Curriculum is a set of planned learning experiences, delineated from a framework of expectations at the goal or outcome level that represents important knowledge, skills, and concepts to be learned. Differentiated curriculum units of study already have been designed and tested for effectiveness in language arts, or units may be developed by teachers to use in gifted instruction.

Differentiation of curriculum for gifted learners is the process of adapting and modifying curriculum structures to address these characteristics and needs more optimally. Thus curriculum goals, outcomes, and activities may be tailored for gifted learners to accommodate their needs. Typically, this process involves the use of the strategies of acceleration, complexity, depth, and creativity in combination.

Instruction is the delivery system for teaching that comprises the deliberate use of models, strategies, and supportive management techniques. For gifted learners, inquiry strategies such as problem-based learning and creative problem solving, and critical-thinking models such as Paul's reasoning model, constitute instructional differentiation when used in a flexible grouping approach in the regular classroom.

Rigor and relevance suggest that the curriculum experiences planned for advanced learners be sufficiently challenging yet provided in real-world contexts that matter to learners at the particular stage of development.

Streamlining is a process to shorten the amount of time that advanced students spend on basic material, even after their functional level is ascertained. Thus compressing the content into larger chunks of learning becomes the task for teachers in order to accommodate advanced student learning pace and rate.

Talent trajectory is used to describe the school span development of advanced learners in their area of greatest aptitude from K–12. It is linked to developmental stages from early childhood through adolescence and defines key interventions that aid in the talent development process, specific to the subject area and desired career path.

Teacher quality refers to the movement at all levels of education to improve the knowledge base and skills of classroom teachers at P–12 levels, which is necessary for effective instruction for advanced students. It is the basis for a redesign of teacher education standards and a rationale for examining P–12 student outcomes in judging the efficacy of higher education programs for teachers. Policy makers are committed to this issue in improving our P–16 education programs.

Appendix B
Evidence-Based Practices
in Gifted Education

Evidence-based practices that inform the teacher preparation and programming standards in gifted education relate to assessment, curriculum, instruction, and grouping issues, all of which are embedded within the CCSS. These practices have an extensive research base. (*Editor's note*: The full references for the citations below can be found in the research base that accompanies the NAGC–CEC Teacher Preparation Standards in Gifted Education, available online at http://www.nagc.org/index.aspx?id=1880.)

Assessment of Individual Characteristics and Needs

- Because of their advanced cognitive functioning, internal locus of control, motivation, and talents, teachers need to provide intellectual challenge in their classrooms to gifted and talented students (Ablard & Tissot, 1998; Barnett & Durden, 1993; Carter, 1985; Gross, 2000; McLauglin & Saccuzzo, 1997; Robinson & Clinkenbeard, 1998; Swiatek, 1993).
- Educators also must be receptive to gifted students' affective needs and sensitive to the social-emotional and cop-

ing needs of special groups of learners (such as highly gifted, gifted students with disabilities, gifted students from diverse backgrounds, gifted girls, and gifted boys (Albert & Runco, 1989; Ford & Harris, 2000; Coleman, 2001; Cross, Stewart, & Coleman, 2003; Gross, 2003; Kennedy, 1995; Peterson, 2003; Shaunessy & Self, 1998; Swiatek & Dorr).

- Gifted students' cultural, linguistic, and intellectual differences should be considered when planning instruction and differentiating curriculum (Boothe & Stanley, 2004).
- Educators need to use preassessment and ongoing assessment to adjust instruction that is consistent with the individual student's progress (Reis, Burns, & Renzulli, 1992; Winebrenner, 2003).
- Assessments used to document academic growth include authentic tasks, portfolios, and rubrics and performance-based assessments (Siegle, 2002; Treffinger, 1994; VanTassel-Baska, 2002).
- The results of progress assessments can be used to adjust instruction including placement in appropriate group learning settings and academic acceleration (Feldhusen, 1996; Kulik, 1992).

Instruction

- Teachers need to use metacognitive and higher level thinking strategies in the content areas and activities that address the gifted students' areas of interest and foster research skills (Anderson & Krathwohl, 2001; Center for Gifted Education, 2000; Elder & Paul, 2003; Hébert, 1993; Johnsen & Goree, 2005; Moon, Feldhusen, & Dillon, 1994; VanTassel-Baska, Avery, Little, & Hughes, 2000).
- Educators should develop gifted students' use of cognitive strategies and encourage deliberate training in spe-

cific talent areas (Bloom & Sosniak, 1981; Ericcson & Charness, 1994; Feldman, 2003).

- Technology can be used in independent studies to access mentors and electronic resources and to enroll in advanced classes (Cross, 2004; Ravaglia, Suppes, Stillinger, & Alper, 1995; Siegle, 2004).

Curriculum

- In the classroom, curricular modifications for gifted students include acceleration, enrichment, grouping, problem-based learning, curriculum compacting, tiered lessons, independent study, and specific curriculum models (Brody, 2004; Betts & Neihart, 1986; Colangelo, Assouline, & Gross, 2004; Gallagher & Stepien, 1996; Gentry, 1999; Johnsen & Goree, 2005; Kulik & Kulik, 1992; Milgram, Hong, Shavit, & Peled, 1997; Renzulli & Reis, 2004; Rogers, 2003; Southern & Jones, 1991; Tomlinson, 2002; Tomlinson, et al., 2001; VanTassel-Baska & Little, 2003).
- Models emphasize the need for considering students' interests, environmental and natural catalysts, curriculum differentiation, and the development of higher level thinking skills (Elder & Paul, 2003; Gagné, 1995; Renzulli & Reis, 2003; Tomlinson & Cunningham-Eidson, 2003).
- When designing a differentiated curriculum, it is essential to develop a scope and sequence and align national, state or provincial, and/or local curricular standards with the differentiated curriculum (Maker, 2004; VanTassel-Baska & Johnsen, 2007; VanTassel-Baska & Stambaugh, 2006).
- Specific curricula have been designed for gifted students and include affective education, leadership, domain-specific studies, and the arts (Clark & Zimmerman, 1997;

Nugent, 2005; Parker & Begnaud, 2003; VanTassel-Baska, 2003a).

- Educators should integrate academic and career guidance into learning plans for gifted students, particularly those from diverse backgrounds (Cline & Schwartz, 2000; Ford & Harris, 1997).
- Differentiated curricula results in increased student engagement, enhanced reasoning skills, and improved habits of mind (VanTassel-Baska, Avery, Little, & Hughes, 2000).
- When individuals from diverse backgrounds are provided challenging curricula, their abilities and potential are more likely to be recognized (Ford, 1996; Ford & Harris, 1997; Mills, Stork, & Krug, 1992).

Environment

- Working in groups with other gifted students and mentors can yield academic benefits and enhance self-confidence and communication skills (Brody, 1999; Davalos & Haensly, 1997; Grybe, 1997; Pleiss & Feldhusen, 1995; Torrance, 1984).
- Working under a successful mentor in their area of interest can foster personal growth, leadership skills, and high levels of learning (Betts, 2004; Brody, 1999; Davalos, & Haensly, 1997; Feldhusen & Kennedy, 1988; Grybe, 1997; Pleiss & Feldhusen, 1995; Torrance, 1984).
- Other learning situations that support self-efficacy, creativity, and lifelong learning include early college entrance programs, talent searches, competitions, problem-based learning, independent play, independent study, and the International Baccalaureate Program (Betts, 2004; Boothe, Sethna, Stanley, & Colgate, 1999; Christophersen & Mortweet, 2003; Gallagher, 1997; Johnsen & Goree, 2005; Rotigel & Lupkowski-Shoplik,

1999; Olszewski-Kubilius, 1998; Poelzer & Feldhusen, 1997; Riley & Karnes, 1998).

- Three factors need to be present for students to develop their talents: (a) above-average ability and motivation; (b) school, community, and/or family support; and (c) acceptance by peers in the domain of talent (Bloom, 1985; Csikszentmihalyi, 1996; Gagné, 2003; Renzulli, 1994; Siegle & McCoach, 2005).

Appendix C
Research Support for the Effort

The research support for the differentiation of the Common Core State Standards for English Language Arts to respond to the needs of the gifted is contained in several studies that have been conducted with both gifted and typical learners in classrooms across the country. Researchers suggest that using a differentiated curriculum and instructional plan designed for the gifted benefits both groups with respect to elevated learning in core language arts areas.

Feng, A. X., VanTassel-Baska, J., Quek, C., Bai, W., & O'Neill, B. (2005). A longitudinal assessment of gifted students' learning using the Integrated Curriculum Model (ICM): Impacts and perceptions of the William & Mary language arts and science curriculum. *Roeper Review, 27,* 78–83.

Abstract: The purpose of this study was to evaluate the effects of the William & Mary language arts and science curriculum, designed around the Integrated Curriculum Model (ICM), in a northeastern suburban school district. The sample consisted of 973 students in grades 3–9. The effect size ranged from .52 to 1.38, and the overall academic growth increased in all of the assessed domains. The results suggested that repeated usage of the William & Mary units yielded an increase in achievement in all tested areas of the language arts.

Kanevsky, L. (2011). Deferential differentiation: What types of differentiation do students want? *Gifted Child Quarterly, 55,* 279–299.
Abstract: Deferential differentiation occurs when the curriculum modification process defers to students' preferred ways of learning rather than relying on teachers' judgments. The preferences of 416 students identified as gifted (grades 3–8) for features of differentiated curriculum recommended for gifted students were compared with those of 230 students not identified as gifted. While thinking of their favorite school subject, they responded to the 110 items on the Possibilities for Learning survey. Most and least popular items are reported in nine thematic categories (pace, collaborative learning, choice, curriculum content, evaluation, open-ended activities, expert knowledge, teacher/student relationship, and sharing learning). Self-pacing, choice of topic, and choice of workmates were most popular with students in both groups. Compared with nonidentified students, more of the students identified as gifted wanted to learn about complex, extracurricular topics and authentic, sophisticated knowledge and interconnections among ideas; to work with others *some of the time*; and to choose the format of the products of their learning. More students identified as gifted also disliked waiting for the rest of the class and asking for help. Overall, the groups' preferences differed in degree rather than kind, and reflected cognitive abilities frequently cited as distinguishing characteristics of learners with high ability.

Mills, C. J., Stork, E. J., & Krug, D. (1992). Recognition and development of academic talent in educationally disadvantaged students. *Exceptionality, 3,* 165–180.
Abstract: Thirty-six students who scored average on standardized achievement tests and were economically disadvantaged

were provided with a program to enhance their mathematics or language arts ability. Twenty-eight students served as a comparison group and received no treatment. After the intervention, the majority of students in the treatment group qualified for academically gifted programs.

Reis, S. M., Eckert, R. D., Fogarty, E. A., Little, C. A., Housand, A. M., Sweeny, S. M., & Sullivan, E. E. (2009). *Joyful reading: Differentiation and enrichment for successful literacy learning*. San Francisco, CA: Jossey-Bass.

Abstract: The Schoolwide Enrichment Model—Reading (SEM-R) is described, with each of the three phases of implementation outlined. This work is geared toward informing teachers how to stimulate interest in reading among students, cultivate an environment that supports students' independent reading, and challenge students to connect interests from texts to creative learning projects. The text also provides guidance in conducting individual student conferences to determine students' comprehension, interest, and areas for continued development and growth based on reading proficiency. A DVD illustrating implementation of SEM-R is included with the text.

Roe, M. F. (2010). The ways teachers do the things they do: Differentiation in middle level literacy classes. *Middle Grades Research Journal, 5,* 139–152.

Abstract: In this qualitative study, the author explored the concept of differentiation in urban, suburban, and rural language arts classrooms. The overall goal of understanding how differentiation occurred in these classrooms led to the following specific intentions: (a) to identify teachers' understandings of differentiation, (b) to understand their implementation of differentiated instruction for their students, especially those who underachieve or those for whom English is their second language, across an academic year, and (c) to understand students' and teachers' views of the challenges and successes of differentiation attempts. Using data collected from the classrooms of nine teachers and across

135 classroom observations and interviews with students and teachers, the author unveiled the following attributes linked to these teachers' differentiation practices: (a) differentiation is more than a classroom event, (b) the classroom climate contributes to differentiation options and practices, (c) differentiation entails attention to affective and cognitive variations, and (d) activities drive differentiation practices.

Swiatek, M. A., & Lupkowski-Shoplik, A. (2000). Gender differences in academic attitudes among gifted elementary school students. *Journal for the Education of the Gifted, 23,* 360–377.

Abstract: This study examined gender differences in attitudes toward academic subjects in 2,089 gifted students in grades 3–6. Observed gender differences were consistent with those found in research with older students. Grade level differences suggest that attitudes toward several academic areas become more negative with age. Attitudes were not related to tested academic ability.

VanTassel-Baska, J., Avery, L. D., Little, C., & Hughes, C. (2000). An evaluation of the implementation of curriculum innovation: The impact of the William & Mary units on schools. *Journal for the Education of the Gifted, 23,* 244–272.

Abstract: Based on focus groups, interviews, documents, and classroom observations of schools implementing the William & Mary language arts and science curricula, it was found that students, teachers, parents, and administrators observed increased student engagement in class, enhanced reasoning skills, and the improvement of habits of mind—including metacognition.

VanTassel-Baska, J., & Bracken, B. (2009). A longitudinal study of enhancing critical thinking and reading comprehension in Title I classrooms. *Journal for the Education of the Gifted, 33,* 7–37.

Abstract: To measure gains in reading comprehension and critical thinking in Title I schools, the researchers conducted a longitudinal study of William & Mary language arts units over a

3-year period. Using six different school districts, 2,771 students in grades 3–5 participated in the study. The results indicated that both the treatment and control groups made statistically significant gains in critical thinking. Although the differences between the two groups were not overwhelming, the scores favored the treatment group.

VanTassel-Baska, J., Johnson, D. T., Hughes, C. E., & Boyce, L. N. (1996). A study of language arts curriculum effectiveness with gifted learners. *Journal for the Education of the Gifted, 19*, 461–480.

Abstract: This study examined the effects of a 40-hour language arts curriculum unit on elementary students in grades 4–6 in selected school districts. The experimental groups improved significantly in all three dimensions of the performance-based assessments: writing, grammar, and syntactic forms and functions. The authors conclude that more targeted curriculum intervention that is aligned with specific assessments needs to occur in classrooms for gifted students.

VanTassel-Baska, J., & Little, C. A. (Eds.). (2009). *Content based curriculum for gifted learners* (2nd ed.). Waco, TX: Prufrock Press.

Abstract: Research-based curriculum models, based on effectiveness studies in science, social studies, and language arts are discussed based on the Integrated Curriculum Model and consequent effectiveness studies related to the model and curriculum for gifted students. A chapter with relevant examples for each core content area as well as an outline of the Integrated Curriculum Model is included.

VanTassel-Baska, J., & Stambaugh, T. (2006). A pathway to advanced literacy development for children of poverty. *Gifted Child Today, 29*, 58–63.

Abstract: This article reports the efficacy of using the *Jacob's Ladder* program with Title I students in order to elevate their reading comprehension skills to the level of critical reading and thinking. The program has shown significant growth for such students at elementary levels and suggests that both higher level questions and activities promote such growth.

VanTassel-Baska, J., Zuo, L., Avery, L. D., & Little, C. A. (2002). A curriculum study of gifted-student learning in the language arts. *Gifted Child Quarterly, 46,* 30–44.

Abstract: Forty-six schools from 17 public school districts and one private school provided student data for this quasiexperimental study. Receiving language arts instruction in either a treatment or control group were 2,189 gifted students in grades 2–8. Students in treatment groups received instruction organized around the Integrated Curriculum Model from teachers trained in the curriculum materials. Overall, the results showed that the William & Mary units produced significant gains for gifted learners in higher order thinking and performance in core language arts areas.

About the Authors

Claire E. Hughes, Ph.D., is an associate professor at the College of Coastal Georgia in an integrated elementary/special education teacher preparation program. Dr. Hughes was recently a Visiting Fellow at Oxford. Author of two books on high-functioning autism, her research areas include twice-exceptional children, cognitive interventions, and Response to Intervention.

Todd Kettler, Ph.D., is an assistant professor in the Department of Educational Psychology at the University of North Texas. He has been a teacher of gifted students and a gifted program director. In his current role, he teaches graduate courses in gifted education.

Elizabeth Shaunessy-Dedrick, Ph.D., is an associate professor of gifted education in the Department of Special Education at the University of South Florida. Her research addresses the social-emotional development of students in International Baccalaureate and Advanced Placement courses, representation of underserved populations of the gifted (primarily English language learners and students from economically challenged

backgrounds). She teaches graduate courses in gifted education and serves as an associate editor of the *Journal of Advanced
Academics*.

Joyce VanTassel-Baska, Ed.D., is the Smith Professor
Emerita at the College of William & Mary, where she developed
a graduate program and a research and development center in
gifted education. Formerly, she initiated and directed the Center
for Talent Development at Northwestern University. She has
also served as the state director of gifted programs for Illinois, as
a regional director of a gifted service center in the Chicago area,
as coordinator of gifted programs for the Toledo, OH, public
school system, and as a teacher of gifted high school students in
English and Latin. Dr. VanTassel-Baska has published widely,
including 29 books and more than 550 referenced journal articles, book chapters, and scholarly reports. Her major research
interests are on the talent development process and effective
curricular interventions with the gifted.